OAKWOOD REMINISCENCES SERIES

CW00646522

Woodford Halse

A Railway Community

by
Ruth Irons
&
Stanley C. Jenkins

THE OAKWOOD PRESS

© Oakwood Press, Ruth Irons & Stanley C. Jenkins 1999

British Library Cataloguing in Publication Data
A Record for this book is available from the British Library
ISBN 0 85361 529 2

Typeset by Oakwood Graphics.
Repro by Ford Graphics, Ringwood, Hants.
Printed by The Witney Press, Witney, Oxon.

There's a flutter at St Pancras, there's a bustle at King's Cross,
They are posting bills and tearing time sheets down,
There's uneasiness at Euston in the office of the 'boss',
For the Central is a-coming to town.

They spoiled the Rugby Polo-ground, they cast their eyes on Lord's
They bridged the great Nor' Western's 4-fold track
They tapped the Midland's coal preserves, and now it's on the boards,
'From Manchester to Marylebone and back'.

On the crowded lines of Derby, 'mid the busy town of Notts,
Thro' the villages and pastures of the Shires,
There's another whistle sounding, and to snug selected spots,
They are sending TRAIN ON LINE along the wires.

Then let them come with all their strength,
we're ready for the race, Be it dining car, or cattle, fish or coal,
Green, Red and Black we're waiting, let their monsters make the pace,
And three of us will race them to the goal.

For it's hard to beat the Northern when the eight-foot single hums, And the Midland
racers 'fly' in spite of weight,
And it's hard to beat Nor' Western, when a big Crewe compound comes,
With just a dozen bogie-cars for freight!

So clear the line before us, drop your signal, set us free,
We are 'blowing off' and chafing at delay,
And let the Central do its best, the country soon shall see
Which one of us will show the rest the way.

A.B.S.

Title page: The entrance to Woodford Halse station on 7th July, 1966.   *R.M. Casserley*

Published by The Oakwood Press (Usk), P.O. Box 13, Usk, Mon., NP15 1YS.
E-Mail: oakwood-press@dial.pipex.com
Website: http://ds.dial.pipex.com/oakwood-press

Contents

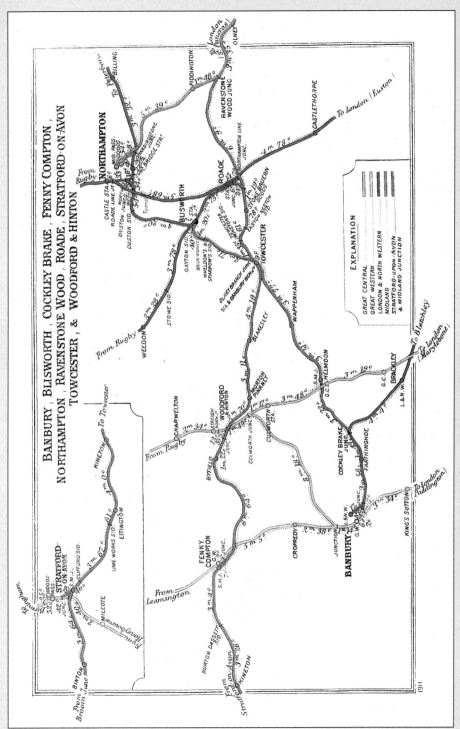

Woodford Halse area as shown in the Railway Clearing House Junction Diagrams book of 1912.

Preface

This publication originated as a local history project based upon Ruth Irons' intimate knowledge of her native village of Woodford Halse, in Northamptonshire. In its original form, the manuscript was, by any definition, an excellent local study, with much interest for railway historians. The publishers felt, however, that the appeal of the book would be widened if the railway content could be increased, and I was therefore asked to add some additional detail concerning the origins of the Great Central Railway (GCR). The result is a four chapter history of the railway community at Woodford Halse. Ruth Irons' original material, with its solid background in social history, has contributed much detail to Chapter One, which deals with the origins of the GCR and its impact on Woodford Halse, while Chapter Two covers the operation and infrastructure of the station, junctions and sidings at this once-busy Great Central location. Chapter Three, in contrast, is a largely personal memoir of life in the railway village. Finally, Chapter Four examines various aspects of village life in greater detail, with particular reference to education, religion and politics.

The Great Central Railway is in many ways a neglected line, and it is hoped that this new volume will fill a gap that has hitherto existed in terms of the social history of the GCR. This is not a history of trains or locomotives, but it is impossible to think of Woodford Halse without reference to the great artery of communication that dominated the life of the community for the span of a human lifetime from the 1890s until the 1960s. All is gone now, but Ruth Irons' personal testimony stands as a tribute to the railway and the men who served its needs.

Stanley C. Jenkins
Witney
Oxfordshire

The staff of the wagon shops about 1900. Sixty men were employed in the Carriage and Wagon Department. *Ruth Irons' Collection*

My father, Wilfrid Irons, 1887-1946. *Ruth Irons' Collection*

Introduction

In the days of the great steam railways, the parish where I was born changed in the space of a few years from a quiet rural community to a busy railway centre. When I arrived on the scene in 1917, the enterprise was almost two decades old. As natural as the air I breathed, was the sight and sound of trains roaring along the high embankment that passed through the centre of our parish like a great throbbing artery. To spend my childhood in such a place, and at such a remarkable time in our history of the parish, was a unique experience. Who could have foreseen that our way of life would last little more than the span of a man's lifetime? Certainly not the railwaymen and their families who came from all parts of the British Isles to live and work there, my father among them.

Our lives were dominated by the railway, and yet, with a child's intuition I was always very conscious and appreciative of the evidence of the village as it used to be, before the railway came to change things for ever. The old ironstone cottages and farms were still there as they had been for centuries, and the pleasant Northamptonshire countryside surrounding the parish was full of interest. My sister and I, with friends from the village, wandered for miles, unmolested in that less violent and more innocent age.

In sharp contrast was the busy, vigorous life of the railway community, where, with the exception of those who worked on the land, tradesmen, and a handful of professional people, nearly all the men were employed in some capacity by the railway company. Perhaps it was those splendid machines, the steam engines, which engendered in some way an enthusiasm for the work, but in the 1920s and 1930s there was truly a feeling that we were all taking part in a tremendous enterprise.

The work of a railwayman was hard, and often hazardous, but so long as the company's rules were obeyed, it was safe employment, or so it seemed to us then. The streets of terraced red brick houses, built for the employees, were not beautiful, but in their day they were considered very comfortable, with water closets, gas lighting, and many amenities not enjoyed by former inhabitants of the old cottages. There was a row of shops, and even at one time a music hall, of which I shall write more later. So all in all, we had the best of both worlds, urban facilities in the midst of rural surroundings.

There were those who said, when finally the railway closed in the sixties, that Woodford would become a ghost village, but this did not happen. Some families left of course, to seek employment elsewhere, but many stayed and commuted to the nearby towns of Banbury, Daventry and Northampton. New estates were built, and the population increased.

Some traces of the railway were removed, for instance the engine shed and wagon shop, familiar landmarks, were demolished, and the embankment lowered, but the core of the village looks today very much as it did half a century ago. Yet the common purpose which governed the lives of most of its inhabitants has gone for ever.

It is no surprise to me that today, the era of the steam locomotives still grips man's imagination. I understand so well the feelings of nostalgia that prompt the formation of railway societies, and the opening of small branch lines with equipment lovingly restored, and I can share in the excitement of children as they clamber over the footplates of those giants of yesteryear in railway museums.

Many books have been written on the subject of railway history. In my village the coming of the steam railway brought great social and environmental changes. This book is an attempt to recapture some of the interest and excitement of an extraordinary period in our village history before it fades from living memory.

This book is dedicated with fondest memories to my father and sister.

Ruth Irons
Carterton
Oxfordshire

My sister and I, aged four and seven years.   *Ruth Irons' Collection*

Chapter One

Woodford Halse and the
Construction of the Railway

On the afternoon of 14th May, 1800, William Wordsworth the poet, and his brother John, set out for Yorkshire from their home in the Lake District. For part of the way they were accompanied by their sister Dorothy, who after bidding them a reluctant farewell, returned home alone to the cottage in Grasmere. Later, she wrote in her Journal, 'Came home by Clappersgate; the valley very green, many sweet views up to Rydale head when I could juggle away the fine houses - they disturbed me even more than when I have been happier'.

Often, I have borrowed those two expressive words, and have tried, in my mind, to 'juggle away' all traces of the railway, so that I might see my village as it was in the middle of the 19th century. Only by so doing can we imagine how great were the changes brought by the building of the Great Central Railway through such a remote and peaceful area.

The Setting: Woodford Halse Before the Railway

The scenery in this part of Northamptonshire is not of a spectacular beauty, but it has a quiet rural charm. The land is gently undulating, with clumps of trees and narrow winding lanes which in my childhood were bordered by a profusion of wild flowers. The village of Woodford Halse, my birthplace, stands on an eminence above the River Cherwell, there no more than a stream, since its source is a mere two miles away in neighbouring Charwelton, my mother's birthplace. On its journey to join the Thames, the stream winds its way through the water meadows westwards past the hamlets of Hinton and West Farndon which make up the parish with its charming Latin name, Woodford-cum-Membris. The old buildings which remain today are constructed of mellow brown ironstone which blends so beautifully with the brown soil on which they stand. Only West Farndon, with its ancient water mill and cluster of farms and cottages, is relatively unchanged from the days when my father came as a boy by carrier's cart from his native Daventry to stay with friends there.

I have before me a list of occupations of people who lived in the parish in 1851, and they give a picture of a truly rural community. Apart from two landed proprietors, some scholars, and four schoolmistresses, most of the men and boys were employed on the land, or in allied trades, and there seems to have been a thriving home industry of lace making for those women and girls who were not employed in domestic service. There was even one hat renovator, which indicates that even among the poor, there was a proper regard for appearances! That there was some poverty and deprivation we cannot doubt, for 32 paupers and five paupers' wives are listed.

One old lady who lived in the parish before the railway was built had no doubts about the benefits it brought. When she was interviewed in the 1950s,

West Farndon mill, near the village of West Farndon, to the south-west of Woodford Halse.
Ruth Irons' Collection

An old cottage at Farndon. The combination of thatched roof and local stone walling is typical of local building practice in the Woodford area.   *Ruth Irons' Collection*

The Hare and Hounds public house *c.* 1900. *Ruth Irons' Collection*

The old post office in the High Street, Woodford Halse. *Ruth Irons' Collection*

South Street, Woodford Halse, showing further examples of the local building style. The building, shown in this *circa* 1930 view probably date back to the 17th, or even 16th centuries.

Ruth Irons' Collection

Old Cottage and Bakehouse, Woodford Halse.   *Ruth Irons' Collection*

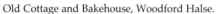

High Street, Woodford Halse. This picturesque street was in effect the centre of the old village.
Ruth Irons' Collection

Old cottages in Scrivens Hill, Woodford Halse. This street was a continuation of School Street.
Ruth Irons' Collection

she stated emphatically, 'Woodford weren't much of a place before the railway came; there were no proper roads, only muddy lanes - no gas or electricity, we had a real hard life!' Considering the primitive conditions prevailing in some of the cottages, her views are understandable, but I cannot help thinking that her opinion was not shared by everyone, and that there must have been some inhabitants who regretted the change from a rural, close-knit community to a busy railway centre.

The Origins of the Great Central Railway

The railway steam engine was a wonderful invention. It evolved, from the time when George Stephenson's *Rocket* attained on its trial run in 1830 the then astonishing speed of 29 mph, into an enormous machine, the embodiment of power and speed. Long ago when I was a small child my father took me to Woodford's engine sheds, and as I stood by the track without the elevation of a platform, the huge engine towering above me filled me with awe; and when I was lifted onto the footplate the shining levers and the smell of oil and grease thrilled me so much that the memory of that day has never faded. I am sure too, that the 'line men' who ministered to, and drove the steam engines, never lost the thrill of being in charge of those powerful machines, for whenever such men met, the talk was always of their experiences up and down the line. It used to embarrass me, when I grew sensitive to those things, that in whatever company we were, sooner or later my father would embark on railway topics. How I wish, in retrospect, that I had listened more carefully to those railwaymen's yarns. They were full of interest and often exciting.

It is hardly surprising then, that in the early years of the 1840s, a kind of Railway Mania spread through the land. Entrepreneurs were quick to see the possibilities offered by the new means of transport, and by 1847 more than a quarter of a million men were toiling to construct over 6,000 miles of railway, while the total expenditure on railway schemes was roughly one-tenth of the national income.

The Manchester, Sheffield & Lincolnshire Railway (MS&L) was one of the first main line companies to be formed, and as its name implies the railway was initially regarded as a trans-Pennine route linking the industrial centres of Sheffield and Manchester. A Sheffield & Manchester Railway company was formed in 1831 but sadly, the promoters of the scheme were unable to raise sufficient capital and the project was abandoned in 1833. Three years later, on 5th May, 1837, a new but substantially-similar scheme known as the Sheffield, Ashton-under-Lyne & Manchester Railway (SA&MR) obtained an Act of Parliament for construction of the hoped for rail link. This revised scheme envisaged a line running from east to west from Sheffield to Manchester via Penistone, Woodhead and Dinting, with a major tunnel through the Pennines at Woodhead.

The first sod of the SA&MR was cut by Lord Wharncliffe on 1st October, 1838, and with Charles Blacker Vignoles (1793-1874) and Joseph Locke (1805-1860) as engineers, major construction was soon under way. The first section of line was opened between Manchester and Godley on 17th December, 1841, and the route was extended to Dinting (then called Glossop) on 24th December, 1842. Meanwhile, work proceeded apace on the difficult Woodhead tunnel section, and after many setbacks the line was ceremonially opened throughout between Sheffield and Manchester on 22nd December, 1845; the first train through Woodhead tunnel was headed by two locomotives, and it arrived in Manchester at around midday as a military band played *See the Conquering Hero Comes*.

Having started its operational life as a trans-Pennine line the Manchester, Sheffield & Lincolnshire Railway soon began to extend its original route at each end. On 1st March, 1848, for example, the Great Grimsby & Sheffield Junction Railway was opened between Grimsby, Habrough and New Holland, while on 1st November, 1848 the line was extended from Habrough to Brigg. In the west, the Manchester South Junction & Altrincham line was opened on 21st July, 1849 as a joint venture between the MS&L and London & North Western railways.

The London Extension Scheme

In the next few years the Manchester, Sheffield & Lincolnshire Railway managed to extend its services to such diverse destinations as Southport, Wigan, Liverpool, Chester, Wrexham and Warrington. However, the MS&L railway remained essentially a northern line, with its system orientated from east-to-west between Grimsby and Merseyside. Manchester, Sheffield & Lincolnshire trains served huge conurbations and thriving industrial areas, but the company's dynamic Chairman, Sir Edward Watkin (1819-1901), was determined to transform the undertaking into a great trunk line, and in order to achieve this aim it was agreed that an entirely new main line would be constructed from Annesley Junction, near Nottingham, to Quainton Road, near Aylesbury. At the latter point, the London Extension would form an end-on junction with the Metropolitan Railway, and Manchester, Sheffield & Lincolnshire trains would thereby be able to reach London by means of running powers over the existing Metropolitan line.

The proposed new line would head southwards via Nottingham, Leicester and Rugby to Quainton Road, from where trains would continue south-eastwards to the Metropolitan Railway terminus at Baker Street. In connection with this scheme, Sir Edward Watkin (who was Chairman of both companies) arranged for MS&L services to have the use of Metropolitan tracks between Quainton Road and Baker Street, the necessary agreement being signed on 18th December, 1890.

The arrangements at the London end of the proposed main line were later modified, and instead of using the Metropolitan station at Baker Street it was agreed that the Manchester, Sheffield & Lincolnshire Railway would build its own terminus at Marylebone, a short section of line being needed between Marylebone and the Metropolitan route at Canfield Place (near Finchley Road) which would be entirely MS&L property.

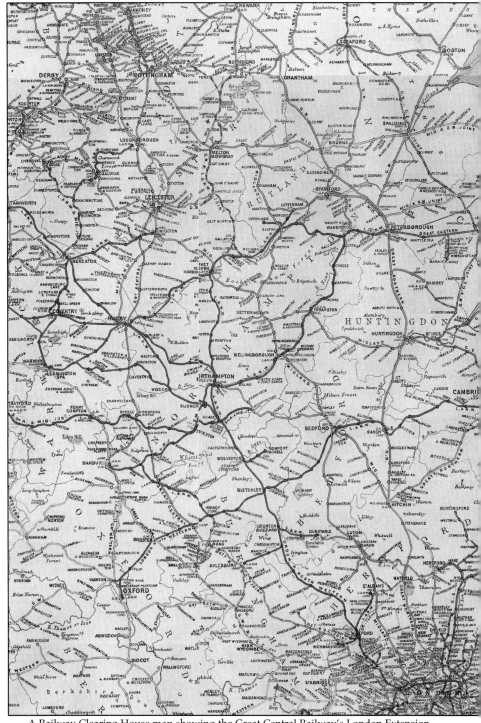

A Railway Clearing House map showing the Great Central Railway's London Extension.

When the MS&L London Extension was first planned there were already three main lines between London and the North, and many commentators argued that there was simply no need for another trunk line.   There was, as a result, considerable opposition to the new scheme, yet despite the difficulties met with at this early stage the scheme went ahead, inspired perhaps by a remark made by the great George Stephenson who, some years before, had stated that a trunk line through Aylesbury would be the best route to the Midlands.

It was all accomplished with remarkable speed. Royal Assent was granted to the Manchester, Sheffield & Lincolnshire Railway London Extension Bill on 28th March, 1893, and the company was thereby empowered to construct over 90 miles of new railway.

Contracts were let in September 1894, and the first sod was ceremonially cut at Alpha Road, near Lord's cricket ground, on 13th November. In a conscious attempt to emulate the very first sod-cutting ceremony on the Woodhead line, the first turf was turned by Lord Wharncliffe, the third Baron, just as his ancestor the first Baron had cut the first sod on the Sheffield, Ashton-under-Lyne & Manchester line, some 56 years before.

The work of construction was soon in full swing, over 9,000 men being employed on the line at one time or another, together with 39 steam navvies each of which could do the work of 100 labourers.   Whole districts were demolished to make way for the new railway in Nottingham and Leicester, while in Nottingham many ancient buildings had to be shored up while tunnelling work continued beneath; on one occasion the navvies broke into the beer cellars of the Old Cross Keys inn, and drank as much alcohol as they could lay their hands on!

Construction in the Woodford Area

So the destiny of Woodford was sealed because, as a result of the lie of the land and its proximity to the towns of Rugby and Leicester, it lay on the proposed route through Aylesbury to the North. It was not our fate to be a quiet little halting place on the line, one of those sleepy small stations which in retrospect seemed always to be bathed in summer sunshine, but a busy railway centre with sheds for 50 engines, a wagon repair shop, and sidings capable of providing standing for 1,000 wagons. Moreover, it would eventually link up with the Great Western Railway (GWR) at Banbury and serve with its freight, the West of England and Wales.

The residents of the parish must have had mixed feelings when the scale of Woodford's participation in the new enterprise first became known. Some, no doubt rejoiced that Woodford would at last 'be put on the map' as it were. Others, the farmers perhaps, would have been dismayed by the interruption in their activities, and the requisition of some of their best acres; and how did the Vicar of St Mary's Church react to the prospect of an alarming increase in the numbers of his flock?

Objections to the railway, whatever their source in the parish were as nothing compared with the furore created at its London terminus. Residents of St John's

Wood were outraged, and the Marylebone Cricket Club talked of the desecration of Lords cricket ground. But progress could not be halted, and the work of building the track went ahead. Cuttings were made, and tunnels were built - including one beneath the MCC ground, which was constructed during the winter months so that it would not interfere with the cricket!

Many years later, on a family outing to London, as we entered the tunnel outside Marylebone station, my father said to me, 'You do realise that we are now travelling *underneath* Lords Cricket Ground!'. So that problem was solved. Another tunnel, because of a dispute with the landowner, had to be made outside the boundary of the parish of Catesby. This was a real feat of engineering. It was 3,000 yards-long, and was constructed under the water shed, so it was named by the railwaymen 'The Wet Tunnel' by reason of its walls dripping with moisture.

On our outings to Rugby and Leicester, the Catesby tunnel provided us children with some magic moments. As the train plunged into the darkness the sound of the wheels passing over the rail joints changed and became muted. There was an acrid smell as steam from the engine forced stale air through windows and doors, and though it might be broad daylight above the tunnel, the lights were switched on in the carriages, giving a cosy, shut-in feeling.

How we admired too, the bridges that spanned the line! They were constructed with blue bricks, and seemed to us so cleverly made. There was a three-arch bridge along the Eydon Road, a short walk from the village, and we used to stand by the parapet above the steep cutting and wait for an express train to pass along. It was exciting to be enveloped in the steam and to feel the ground reverberate beneath our feet. They are countless, the experiences in my childhood which I owe to the work of those labourers, so many years ago.

They were tough men, the navvies employed by the railway company. At first they slept rough under hedges and in barns or outhouses until complaints were made to the parish council who formed a committee to meet the contractors, Messrs T. Oliver & Sons, in an effort to prevent the nuisance their workmen created to the residents of the parish. Eventually the navvies, most of them itinerant workers, and many of them Irish, were housed in huts outside the village near Dairy Farm where there were gravel and sand pits excavated for ballast. For those who required superior lodgings, a hostel was provided in Woodford opposite the Hare & Hounds Inn at the top of Scrivens Hill. Miss Adeline Mary Pym who kept the hostel must have been a lady of a philanthropic turn of mind, for she did much to alleviate the hardships suffered by the navvies.

According to a contemporary account given by an employee at the time, the navvies living in the vicinity of Dairy Farm were kept well supplied with beer, in fact the whole place was undoubtedly run as an illicit beer house. Small wonder then, that when a visit from an exciseman was rumoured, there were many willing helpers to bury the kegs of beer in the banks of the Eydon Road cutting, until the danger had passed.

Some interesting recollections of the building of the railway through Woodford Halse were provided by Mr William Welch, who later took a permanent job with the railway company as a ganger at Willoughby.   He remembered that the first work in the Woodford area commenced in 1895, though activities were suspended during the winter months owing to the severity of the weather; Mr Welch therefore worked for the railway contractors during the summer and returned home to Bugbrooke during the winter to find employment on a farm.

At one time he lodged at Eydon, and could remember the contractors' tank locomotives drawing one open wagon in which the men rode from the bridge on the Eydon to Moreton Pinkney Road to Greenhills Cutting at Culworth.

The navvies were paid from 4¼d. to 5d. per hour, though the specialist tunnel miners may have received a little more; a 'Walking Ganger' travelled up and down the line to check the number of men at work, and he could also hire or fire workers as required, and pay out 'subs'; men could be dismissed at one hour's notice.

Further reminiscences of the work involved during the construction of the railway were supplied by Mr Harry Gardner, who as a youth had been employed as an engine cleaner by the contractors at Charwelton.   He was engaged mainly on night duties, and on one occasion he remembered being told to take charge of four locomotives for the night.   These engines were being used to test the newly-constructed bridges between Annesley Junction and Aylesbury, and Mr Gardner had to tend their fires and ensure that the boilers were kept full; he remembered that one of them was No. 286, which was later depicted in a coloured print displayed in the Bell Inn at Byfield.

Mr Gardner was invited to start work on the railway as a cleaner when the line was opened for traffic at the rate of 2s. 6d. per day, and in this capacity he accompanied the first main line engines into Woodford locomotive depot - the buildings were not then complete, and goods wagons were therefore pressed into service as temporary offices and mess cabins.

Other details of the line under construction can be found in the pages of local newspapers such as the *Northampton Herald*, which on 12th January, 1895 mentioned that the contractors had asked the Daventry Highway Board for sanction to divert a road at Woodford-cum-Membris so that the railway could cross over it at right angles.   The Surveyor was directed to reply that he could not sanction such a diversion (possibly because the powers of the highway board were about to pass to the district council).

On 28th May, 1898 the newspaper referred to Police Constable Charles Ringham, who was described as an additional constable employed by the railway company at Woodford.   A few days later, on 4th June, the paper reported three cases of fighting and bad language at Woodford, while George Howard, a 'railway labourer' of no fixed abode, was charged with stealing codfish from George Oliver, a fish salesman, and two fowls from W. Marriott of the White Hart Hotel; he was sentenced to six weeks' hard labour.

The Completion of the Scheme

The London Extension was substantially complete by 1898, the work of construction having been accomplished in about four years. In the meantime, the Manchester, Sheffield & Lincolnshire Railway had changed its name, a more expansive title being adopted in view of the company's grandiose ambitions; henceforth, the railway would be known as the Great Central Railway, and the words 'GREAT CENTRAL' were soon being applied in full to locomotives and passenger vehicles in readiness for the opening of the line from Annesley to Marylebone.

On 25th June, 1898 the *Northampton Herald* printed a further report on the progress of the scheme with particular reference to Woodford, which would soon be transformed into an important rural junction station on the London Extension. Some of this report is worth quoting in full.

> The new Great Central Railway, which it is expected will be opened shortly, will have an important centre at Woodford Junction. Already, sheds for 48 engines are approaching completion, as well as a shed some 300 feet long for repairing wagons, and a building in which to mend wagon sheets.
>
> A well has been sunk near the station, some 75 feet deep to supply locomotives with water, which is to be pumped up to the sheds some quarter of a mile away by a powerful engine.
>
> There are no less than eight signal boxes in the parish, one of which contains 76 levers. Three are for main line traffic and four for the sidings, which will be extensive, accommodation being provided for standing somewhere about 1,000 wagons.
>
> Woodford is to be a sorting depot, besides which, in addition to the above mentioned, it is quite probable that there will eventually be carriage works there.
>
> On Friday of last week the Directors of the line were conveyed over the route from Quainton Road to Annesley Junction, the train consisting of an engine and tender, and two coaches. They arrived at Woodford station at about 5 o'clock, and made a short stay.
>
> It is expected that the line will shortly be running goods trains, and that passenger trains will run before the year ends.
>
> It is not so many years ago since, to travel by train, Woodford's inhabitants had to go to Weedon or Fenny Compton. Soon they will have a station, at which most trains will call, in their very midst. The new line bids fair to become the best route from the North to London.
>
> Messrs Melcombe Brothers, of Bedford, are building some 200 cottages for the accommodation of the railway company's employees, so that the population will shortly be considerably increased.

On 30th July, 1898 the same newspaper reported that the first coal train had run over the route through Woodford 'on Monday', though the line was not opened for passenger traffic until the following year.

The London Extension was formally opened on 9th March, 1899, when the Rt Hon. Charles T. Ritchie, the President of the Board of Trade, dispatched the official 'First Train' out of Marylebone station behind 4-4-0 locomotive No. 861. Public services began six days later on 15th March, the first express working over the Great Central main line to the North being the 5.15 am from Marylebone, which departed with just four passengers on board.

It was initially hoped that Woodford would be able to celebrate the official opening of the line on 9th March, and just three days previously, on 6th March, the parish council had resolved to instruct their clerk to draw up an address to present to the GCR Directors when their special working reached Woodford station. Unfortunately, the Directors would not stop the 'First Train' even for a minute, though it is believed that the Vicar of Woodford, the Reverend F.A. Smith, was able to thank the railway company formally for the many blessings conferred by the building of the line when he purchased the first ticket from the booking office on 15th March, 1899.

Some Details of the Line

The new main line was, from its inception, in competition with the established lines of the Midland Railway, London & North Western Railway and (to a lesser extent) the Great Northern Railway companies, and all of the major cities on the new GCR route were already served by one or other of the rival lines. Nevertheless, the Great Central route was an impressive example of railway engineering.

Starting from its purpose-built terminus at Marylebone the new line proceeded for a little under two miles to Canfield Place, where trains reached the Metropolitan line. Beyond, the route continued to Quainton Road, where the purely Great Central route resumed; at first GCR trains exercised running powers over the Metropolitan line, but in 1906 the entire line between Harrow and Quainton Road (including the branch lines to Verney Junction, Chesham and Brill) became joint Metropolitan and Great Central property.

Continuing northwards from Quainton the GCR line climbed towards Finmere (54½ miles) at 1 in 176, then dropped down to Brackley (59¼ miles) before climbing once again to the summit near Helmdon (62½ miles from Marylebone). Heading northwards the route continued via Culworth (66 miles), Woodford (69 miles) and Charwelton (71½ miles) to Rugby, some 83¼ miles from London; here, the line was carried across the LNWR line on a girder viaduct.

From Rugby the route continued northwards to Leicester (103 miles), where trains were carried through the town on long stretches of embankment and brick viaducts. At Nottingham (126½ miles) several expensive tunnels were necessary in order that the new line could continue through the built-up areas towards Annesley Junction and the original Manchester, Sheffield & Lincolnshire system with its connections to Sheffield, Bradford, Manchester and a range of other destinations in the North of England.

The new route was characterised by long stretches of 1 in 176 gradient in each direction, and there were numerous civil engineering works including tunnels at Marylebone, Catesby and Nottingham, and viaducts at Brackley, Rugby, Leicester, Nottingham, Bulwell and elsewhere.

The stations were laid out on an 'island' pattern with the running lines on each side, this layout being employed for both large and small stopping places. Although island layouts enabled the railway builders to economise on the number of platforms there were minor difficulties in terms of public access - convenient over or underbridges being used wherever possible with stairways between road and platform levels.

A turn of the century view of Calvert, on the GCR main line some 20¼ miles to the south of Woodford, showing the characteristic island platform arrangement, and the standardised brick buildings. Note the milk dock in the foreground.   *Lens of Sutton*

Finmere station in the early 1930s. Finmere was 54½ miles from Marylebone and 14½ miles to the south of Woodford Halse. It was the only Great Central/LNER station in Oxfordshire. Access to the island platform was via a covered flight of steps from the main A421 road, which passed under the line at the south end of the station.   *D. Jackson Collection*

An early postcard view of Brackley station. Brackley was a slightly larger station, with high level buildings in addition to the usual GCR-type platform buildings.   *D. Jackson Collection*

Helmdon (for Sulgrave) station was 62½ miles from Marylebone and 6½ miles to the south of Woodford Halse. It was a typical London Extension station with the usual island platform layout and standard red brick station buildings.   *D. Jackson Collection*

Culworth station was 66 miles from Marylebone and only three miles to the south of Woodford Halse. It was a standard London Extension station; access was from the adjacent road bridge via the covered stairway that can be seen to the left.   *D. Jackson Collection*

An early view of Woodford Halse, looking north. The Banbury branch platform is visible to the left.   *D. Jackson Collection*

Charwelton, some 2½ miles north of Woodford Halse on the GCR main line, was another typical 'London Extension' station with an island platform and brick buildings. In this case access was arranged from the nearby road overbridge. This Edwardian view shows the station, looking southwards towards Woodford.   *Lens of Sutton*

Another view of Charwelton station, on the GCR main line to the north of Woodford Halse. This view dates from October 1927.   *D. Jackson Collection*

The larger stations were equipped with high level buildings at right angles to the platforms, whereas the smaller stations typically had platform level station buildings with gated entrances at road level.

The railway was built mainly of brick, red brick being used for station buildings, while blue bricks were extensively used for viaducts and bridges. Many of the wayside stations on the London Extension were situated in remote rural areas that offered little immediate opportunity for traffic growth, though the inhabitants of agricultural communities such as Finmere and Charwelton must obviously have welcomed the new means of transport. Woodford station was actually sited between the villages of Woodford Halse and Hinton, for which reason it was known for many years as 'Woodford & Hinton'.

On a minor point of detail it should be mentioned that the first railway to impinge upon the Woodford area was in fact the East & West Junction line, which passed to the south of the village and had been opened on 1st July, 1873. This minor line provided a local service to Stratford-upon-Avon in the west and Blisworth in the east, by means of which the people of Woodford Halse were able to reach the outside world by rail. There was, however, no station in Woodford itself, the nearest stations on the East & West Junction Railway being at Byfield, some two miles to the west, and Moreton Pinkney, about 3½ miles to the south-east.

Interestingly, the East & West Junction line had been used for the transport of materials during the construction of the Great Central route. The blue bricks used for bridge works, for example, were transported from Nuneaton and handed over to the GCR at Woodford West Junction, while the first engine employed by Messrs Olivers was delivered to Moreton Pinkney station and conveyed by road to Greenhills cutting, where it was handed to the contractors. The engine was hauled from Moreton Pinkney behind a traction engine driven by Fred Ward of Woodford, and owned by Parson Smith.

The Great Central station at Rugby.   *D. Jackson Collection*

Chapter Two

The Railway in Operation

Having described the origins of the Great Central London Extension line it would now be appropriate to examine the railway facilities in and around Woodford in greater detail. The following section will therefore describe Woodford station and the surrounding lines as they would have appeared in their heyday.

Woodford Station

Woodford & Hinton station was situated on the Great Central main line a little over 69 miles from Marylebone, and 34 miles south of Leicester. The station was approached via a succession of rising gradients, with lengthy stretches of 1 in 176 between Grendon Underwood Junction and Helmdon summit; thereafter the route descended, again with long stretches of 1 in 176, between Helmdon, Woodford and Leicester.

The station was orientated on a north-to-south alignment, and in accordance with GCR practice on the London Extension, facilities were concentrated on a central island platform, with the main up and down tracks on either side. An additional platform was erected on the western side of the station in connection with the opening of the Banbury branch in June 1900, and there were thus three platform faces in all.

Public access was arranged by means of a covered stairway which ascended from a road underbridge at the north end of the station, and by this means travellers were able to reach the booking office and waiting rooms; there were 54 wooden steps between the road and platform levels.

The main station building was of typical Great Central design. Of brick construction, it contained all of the usual facilities including a general waiting room, ladies' waiting room, booking office, refreshment room, porters' room and toilet accommodation. The main building sported an extensive canopy which gave protection to travellers waiting on both the up and down sides. A lattice girder footbridge was situated at the north end of the platform, and this provided pedestrian access to the Banbury branch platform on the down side of the running lines.

Woodford's goods handling facilities were modest in relation to the size of the station. A relatively small, but well-equipped goods yard was provided on the up, or east side of the running lines, and this contained the usual range of accommodation for coal, minerals, cattle, general merchandise, timber, machinery, and other forms of traffic; a two-ton fixed yard crane was available for use when heavy or bulky consignments were sent by rail.

There were, in addition to the goods sidings in the up yard, a number of marshalling sidings on the down side of the line, and these were extended in the mid-1930s when six more sidings were added. Further expansion came during

An early view of Woodford Halse station, the station nameboard reads 'Woodford & Hinton'.
Ruth Irons' Collection

Woodford Halse station in GCR days. The station nameboard now reads just 'Woodford'. The name was changed to Woodford Halse on 1st November, 1948.   *D. Jackson Collection*

Woodford Halse station, looking south towards Marylebone. *D. Jackson Collection*

Woodford Halse station in BR days around 1962. The Banbury branch platform on the left has now been rebuilt in concrete. *D. Jackson Collection*

A general view of the engine shed at Woodford in BR days. The engines visible are, from left to right, a 'B1' class 4-6-0, a 'V2' class 2-6-2, a pair of 'WD' 2-8-0s, and a BR Standard '4MT' 2-6-0.
D. Matthews/R. Palmer Collection

Woodford Halse station in BR days, looking south *c*. 1962. The top of the stairway can be seen to the left and Woodford No. 4 signal box is visible in the distance. *D. Jackson Collection*

Woodford Halse station in BR days, looking north. The covered stairway can again be seen, while the down sidings are visible in the left distance. *D. Jackson Collection*

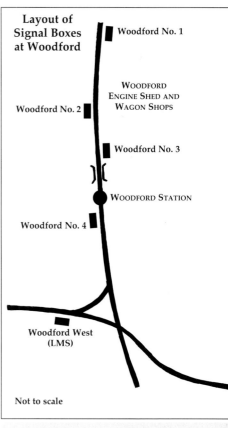

Layout of Signal Boxes at Woodford

Woodford No. 1

WOODFORD ENGINE SHED AND WAGON SHOPS

Woodford No. 2

Woodford No. 3

WOODFORD STATION

Woodford No. 4

Woodford West (LMS)

Not to scale

Above: Woodford No. 1 signal box was the most northerly of Woodford's signal boxes and was located on the up side, it is seen here in a state of dereliction after closure. It was constructed during World War II. The box had control of the up and down main lines and the up and down loops as well as the entry into the new up yard and exit from the new down sidings.   *D. Jackson Collection*

Right: Woodford No. 2 signal box was located on the down side opposite the wagon shops. The box had previously been known as Woodford North Loop. It controlled the up and down main lines and loops, the exit from the new up yard and the entry to the old up yard via the loop, also entry to the new down yard down via the down main or down loop lines. It also controlled the engine shed and wagon shops area.   *D. Jackson Collection*

Woodford No. 3 signal box was sited just north of Woodford Halse station on the up side; it controlled the up and down main lines and loops, the exit from the old up yard, the entry to the old down yard and the entry and exit to the middle road.   *D. Jackson Collection*

Woodford No. 4 signal box was approximately 120 yards south of Woodford station on the down side; it had previously been known as Woodford Central. It controlled the up and down main lines and loops as well as Woodford North Junction which gave access to the ex-S&MJR line to Stratford-upon-Avon.   *Chris Chesterman*

World War II, when two new marshalling yards were added to the north of the station for up and down traffic; the accommodation provided at Woodford was, by that time, capable of handling no less than 3,255 wagons.

Woodford engine shed, which normally housed around 50 locomotives, was sited to the north of the passenger station on the up side of the running lines. The shed building was of brick construction, with a ridge-and-furrow roof; it spanned six parallel tracks, and extensive office and repair facilities were incorporated within the building, while coal and watering facilities were available nearby. In later years, an elevated coaling plant was erected to the south-east of the main shed building.

A large, brick-built building to the south-west of the locomotive shed served as a wagon repair shop. Like the engine shed, this extensive structure had a northlight-pattern roof, and it spanned three parallel sidings. The area between the engine and wagon repair sheds was occupied by a smaller building with a clerestory roof which was used for the repair of wagon sheets, and to the right of this a siding gave access to a tall sheerlegs and hoist, by means of which heavy components could be raised during repair operations.

In addition to these major buildings the locomotive yard was liberally provided with a number of single-storey brick offices and mess rooms which, from their characteristic flat-roofed appearance, obviously dated from the 1930s or 1940s. Water for the engines was obtained from wells, a new shaft being sunk in 1936 to supply the 65,000,000 gallons that were needed each year; this new supply was pumped electrically at the rate of 5,000 gallons per hour.

A general view of the engine shed in BR days, looking north. Note the sheerlegs to the left. *D. Jackson Collection*

The Connecting Lines

Although Woodford & Hinton was a rural station in a comparatively remote area, it was operationally important in that it was both a busy junction and the site of an important motive power depot. Two lines diverged from the main GCR route in the immediate vicinity, the Great Central Banbury branch, and a short spur to the East & West Junction Railway near Byfield.

The Banbury branch provided an important connection between the Great Central Railway and the neighbouring Great Western Oxford to Birmingham main line. It was built by the GCR at Great Western expense under an agreement between the two companies, and opened for goods traffic on 1st June, 1900, and for passengers on 13th August, 1900. All services were provided by the GCR, though trains ran over the GWR for 1 miles 13 chains in order to terminate in the Great Western station at Banbury.

The branch, which was double track throughout, left the Great Central London Extension at Culworth Junction some 1¾ miles, to the south of Woodford station, and ran south-westwards across the high wolds of Northamptonshire and North Oxfordshire to join the GWR at Banbury Junction. Intermediate stopping places were provided at Eydon Road and Chalcombe Road Platform, and the distance from Woodford & Hinton to Banbury was 11 miles.

The Byfield spur, in contrast, was merely a short curve extending south-westwards from the Great Central at the southern end of Woodford station and joining the East & West Junction line at Woodford West Junction. The spur, which was double-tracked, was 47 chains in length, and it was opened in March 1899. There was at one time a similar spur on the south side of Woodford West Junction which allowed through running onto the GCR in a southerly direction, but this was abandoned as a through connection in October 1900, and its site was later occupied by sidings.

A local branch train at Woodford during the early years of the 20th century.

Lens of Sutton

Robinson 4-4-0 No. 110 provides the backdrop for this group photograph. Young fireman
Wilfrid Irons is seen second from left.   *Ruth Irons' Collection*

A visitor to Woodford was this ex-NER 0-6-0, this photograph was taken by my father's fireman
in 1923.   *Ruth Irons' Collection*

The East & West Junction line was much older than the GCR London Extension, having been authorised on 23rd June, 1864 and completed throughout from Towcester to Stratford-upon-Avon on 1st July, 1873. On 1st August, 1908 the East & West Junction Railway was formally amalgamated with two smaller companies to form the Stratford-upon-Avon & Midland Junction Railway, and in 1923 the entire line became part of the LMS system.

The presence of the Banbury and Byfield lines contributed an atmosphere of bustle and activity at Woodford that would otherwise not have existed. The Banbury line in particular was a major artery for through passenger and freight traffic between the Midlands and North of England and the south coast, while the Byfield spur provided a convenient connection for tourist traffic between London and Stratford-upon-Avon. In the latter context it is interesting to recall that through coaches were once provided between Marylebone and Stratford via Woodford and Byfield, the distance from Marylebone and the GCR route being only 93¼ miles compared with 102¾ miles via the rival Great Western route from Paddington.

The Locomotives

For locomotive enthusiasts, Woodford & Hinton was always a place of considerable interest. It was in many ways the operational hub of the London Extension, and in addition to the many non-stop express and semi-fast services between London, Sheffield and the North there were local trains to Marylebone, Banbury and Nottingham, through trains to the South via Banbury and endless processions of coal and freight trains, many of which were handed over to the Great Western at Banbury.

The first main line trains between Marylebone and the North were hauled by a range of newly-designed locomotives which were remarkable for the elegance of their proportions and the care lavished on their external appearance. The standard main line engines in the earliest years were 4-4-0s built to the design of Harry Pollitt, the GCR locomotive engineer, and introduced in 1897. The first example of this type was No. 268, while sister engine No. 269 was chosen to haul the inaugural train over the London Extension in 1899.

In 1900 Harry Pollitt retired from service and was succeeded as locomotive engineer by John G. Robinson. A new 4-4-0 design - the celebrated '1020', '11B' or 'Sir Alexander' class - was introduced at the end of the following year; these engines were similar to their Pollitt predecessors, and they were regarded by many as among the most handsome locomotives ever built.

J.G. Robinson continued to design ever-larger locomotives for the GCR line, all of which exhibited a distinct family likeness. In 1903, for example, he introduced his first Atlantic 4-4-2s, Nos. 192 and 194, together with two 4-6-0s, numbered 195 and 196. Further 'Atlantics 'appeared at intervals between 1904 and 1906, and there were eventually 31 of these exceptionally good-looking engines, 27 of which were designated class '8B' while a further four comprised class '8D' - the latter group being three-cylinder compounds.

Robinson 2-8-0 goods engine No. 6312.

Real Photographs

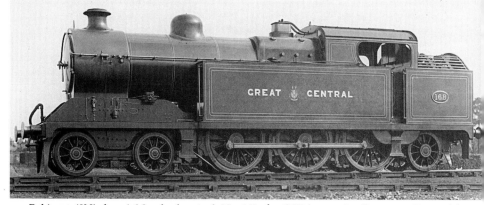

Robinson '9N' class 4-6-2 suburban tank No. 168; the GCR locomotive livery was Brunswick green with purple-brown frames.

Real Photographs

Robinson Atlantic No. 363, in Great Central livery. Like the 'Directors' the Robinson 4-4-2s worked on the Great Central line for many years. No. 363 was built in 1906 as a class '8B'. It was numbered 5363 by the LNER, and initially painted in full apple green livery. Later, however, the Atlantics were painted in lined black. They became class 'C4' under LNER auspices.

Real Photographs

Additional 4-6-0s continued to be built until 1921 for both passenger and mixed traffic duties, while in 1913 Robinson introduced his famous 'Director' class 4-4-0s, the first 10 engines being turned out in that year, to be followed by an additional batch of 11 in 1920 (with a further 28 engines appearing under LNER auspices in 1924).

All of these engines sported the Great Central company's attractive locomotive livery of dark green lined in black and white, with dark purple-red underframes, though goods engines appeared in a lined black colour scheme.

Other locomotives seen in and around Woodford & Hinton in the early years of the century included Robinson '9K' and '9L' class 4-4-2Ts, Robinson '9N' class 4-6-2Ts, Robinson '9J' class 0-6-0s, Robinson '8K' class 2-8-0s, and Parker, Pollitt and Robinson 0-6-2Ts.

The engines employed at the southern end of the Great Central system tended to be of relatively new construction - the London Extension was, after all, something of a showpiece! There was, nevertheless, at least one older class in regular use in the Woodford area, the engines in question being ancient Sacré outside-framed 2-4-0Ts which had been adapted for push-pull operation for use on the Banbury branch and other secondary services.

Many Great Central locomotives were known by a range of curious nicknames, which appear to have gained widespread acceptance among local railwaymen. Indeed, at least one former footplateman recalled that, when starting his career in the locomotive department, he was told to acquaint himself with these appellations because his colleagues would regularly use the nicknames when referring to the different classes of engine. The '8B' class Atlantics, for example, were popularly known as 'Jersey Lillies' because their curvaceous bodies were said to remind people of the actress Lillie Langtry!

The '9N' class 4-6-2Ts became known as 'Coronations' because they were introduced in George V's Coronation year of 1911, while the '1B' class 2-6-4Ts were designated 'Crabs' because of their somewhat ungainly appearance. The Robinson '9J' 0-6-0s were universally known as 'Pom-Poms' because their staccato exhaust beats were said to resemble a type of exploding machine gun shell that had been fired at British forces during the Boer War from Maxim guns. Winston Churchill (then a war correspondent) clearly remembered 'the shellfiring Maxim . . . and its little shells, discharged with an ugly thud, thud, thud' and exploding with 'startling bangs on all sides'.

The Robinson '11B' class 4-4-0s were also named after these machine gun shells, being known as 'Passenger Pom-Poms', or 'Bogie Pom-Poms', or (in some areas) 'Pom-Pom Bogies'. Other well-known names for Great Central locomotives included 'Square-Toppers' for the Pollitt '11A' class 4-4-0s, 'Fish Engines' for the Robinson '8' class 4-6-0s, and 'Imminghams' for the Robinson '8F' class 4-6-0s .

A busy scene showing Parker 'N5' class 0-6-2T No. 5768 at Woodford. These engines were used on a range of duties including yard shunting and local freight or passenger work.

Ruth Irons' Collection

Ex-Great Northern Large Atlantic No. 3293 is seen on shed at Woodford on 13th December, 1936. This locomotive was built at Doncaster in 1905 to the design of H.A. Ivatt. The Ivatt Large Atlantics became LNER class 'C1'.

D. Jackson Collection

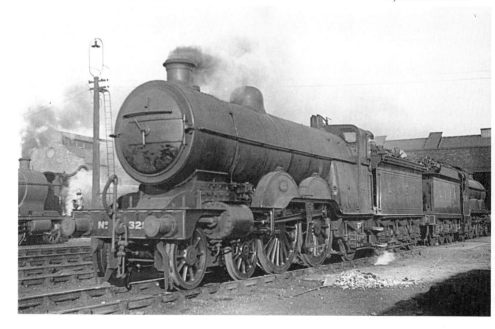

Post-Grouping Changes

The settled conditions that had pertained prior to World War I were replaced by a very different economic situation after 1918; like all railways, the Great Central emerged from the war in a run-down condition, the four years of conflict having resulted in reduced amenities, deferred maintenance and decelerated train services. In response to this situation the Government decided to group the main line railways into four large undertakings, this decision being seen as an acceptable alternative to outright nationalisation. Accordingly, in 1923, the Great Central Railway was merged with the Great Northern, Great Eastern, North Eastern, North British and other companies to form the aptly-named London & North Eastern Railway.

The Grouping did not produce any immediate effects in places such as Woodford & Hinton, and Woodford Shed continued to house large numbers of former Great Central locomotives. The liveries of locomotives and rolling stock were progressively changed to reflect LNER standards, large passenger engines being painted in an apple green colour scheme while goods locomotives and less important passenger and mixed traffic locomotives appeared in LNER black livery.

The LNER also introduced a new alpha-numeric engine identification system based upon locomotive wheel arrangements, 4-6-2 engines being given an 'A' prefix, 4-6-0s receiving a 'B' prefix, and so on. Insofar as this concerned the engines seen at Woodford & Hinton, the small Robinson 4-4-0s became LNER class 'D9', the 'Pom-Pom' 0-6-0s became class 'J11', the Atlantics became class 'C4' and the 0-6-2Ts became class 'N5'. The 'Director' 4-4-0s, meanwhile were designated class 'D10', 'D11' or 'D11/2' (depending on batch), while the 4-4-2 tanks became LNER classes 'C13' or 'C14'.

It the next few years the LNER sent engines from other pre-Grouping companies into the Woodford area, and in this context former Great Northern 'N2' 0-6-2Ts, ex-North British 0-6-0s and ex-Great Eastern 4-4-0s were among the occasional 'foreign' engines seen in the vicinity. New engine classes such as the massive 'V2' 2-6-2s, 'B17' 4-6-0s and 'J39' class 0-6-0s were also employed on the London Extension, though the original Great Central classes survived for many years, and as late as the 1950s there were still significant numbers of former GCR locomotives at Woodford Halse. (In 1950, for example, Woodford shed was still home to five 'N5' class 0-6-2Ts, together with no less than ten 'Pom-Pom' 0-6-0 goods engines!)

One small, but important change carried out under LNER auspices concerned the numbering system for locomotives and rolling stock. In the case of locomotives the former Great Central classes were re-numbered in the 5XXX series, the original GCR numbers being increased by 5,000, so that (for example) Robinson Atlantics 4-4-2 Nos. 192 and 364 became Nos. 5192 and 5364 respectively.

Despite these changes Woodford & Hinton remained a bastion of Great Central influence throughout the 1920s and 1930s, and there is no doubt that the men who worked there continued to think of themselves as Great Central Railwaymen, with their own customs, loyalties and traditions of service.

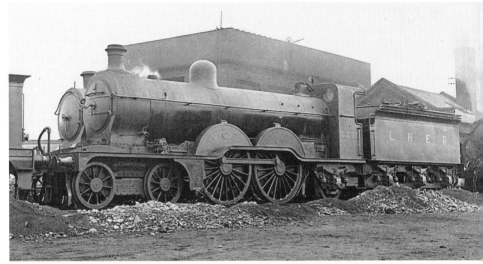

Another ex-Great Northern visitor . Here we see an Ivatt 'C2' class Small Atlantic at Woodford. This engine was one of the inside-cylindered examples.   *D. Jackson Collection*

The first ten 'Directors' (Nos. 429-438) appeared in 1913, but a subsequent batch (Nos. 501-511) were added in 1920; No. 5501 *Mons*, seen here, was the first of the 'Improved Directors' of 1920. 'Directors' worked the 12.15 pm Marylebone to Manchester Express for many years. In LNER days the 'Improved Directors' became class 'D11', whereas the original engines were designated class 'D10'.   *Real Photographs*

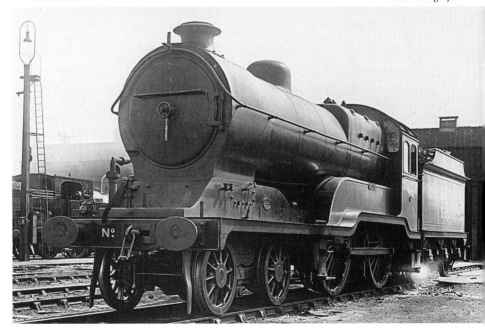

An ex-GCR 'Director' 4-4-0 is seen on Charwelton troughs *c.* 1925. *D. Jackson Collection*

LNER 'B17' class 4-6-0 No. 2847 *Helmingham Hall* at Charwelton on 3rd July, 1937.
D. Jackson Collection

Some Main Line Trains through Woodford, circa 1900-1910

An early morning newspaper train to Manchester was introduced in 1899 as a result of an agreement made between the *Daily Mail* and the Great Central Railway, whereby the railway undertook to convey late editions of the paper to the populous cities of the North and Midlands in time for breakfast reading the following morning. The train stopped at Rugby at 4.27 am and then ran non-stop to Leicester (arr. 4.50 am), Nottingham (arr. 5.20 am) and thence to Sheffield (arr. 6.10 am). The train finally reached Manchester at 7.15 am after a fast run over the intervening 206 miles from Marylebone.

Early morning newspaper traffic was so important that a second 'Newspaper' left Marylebone at 5.15 am, and this working ran non-stop as far as Leicester. Both of the 'Newspapers' also carried passengers.

Other fast trains over the Great Central main line during the early 1900s included the 3.25 pm 'Sheffield Special' and the 6.20 pm dining car train from Marylebone to Leicester, Nottingham, Sheffield and Bradford. In the up direction, the best train of the day was probably the 8.50 am from Sheffield, which called only at Nottingham (arr. 9.35 am) and then ran the 126½ miles from there to Marylebone in 134 minutes.

None of these trains stopped at Woodford at that time, but the station was served by a number of other express or semi-fast services including the 12.15 pm and 4.00 pm workings from Marylebone and the 8.25 am from Manchester to London; the latter train conveyed a through portion from Halifax to Bristol, which was detached at Leicester and called *en route* at Woodford on its way to Banbury and the Great Western system.

These timings varied over the years, and some of the best trains later stopped at Woodford. The trains also became progressively heavier as the Great Central slowly attracted additional travellers from the rival Midland and London & North Western routes from London to the North. However, in the early days of the line some of the fast services consisted of no more than three bogie coaches, though the standard formation in the years before World War I had increased to five vehicles.

There were, in general, around 14 trains each way between Marylebone and the North of England during the early 1900s, including the two early morning 'Newspapers'. Although not all of these stopped at Woodford & Hinton, local travellers benefited from the provision of additional services to and from the Banbury branch, including through workings from Oxford, Bournemouth and Southampton; the 'Bournemouth' included through portions for Liverpool, Manchester and Newcastle, while the Oxford and Southampton services ran through to York. Woodford was also served by local trains to Banbury and elsewhere, and by March 1910 the daily timetable provided 16 workings in the down (northbound) direction, five of which started from the station, together with 17 stopping or terminating services in the up (southbound) direction.

A Note on Great Central Rolling Stock

As mentioned above, when the London Extension was opened for public traffic in 1899 the new route was in open competition with the Midland Railway and other companies, and in order to attract customers from the established lines the Great Central introduced new rolling stock of luxurious design. At a time when many railway companies were content to run trains of short-wheelbase non-corridor stock the Great Central could boast that its main line trains were vestibuled throughout, with restaurant or buffet cars.

The new bogie coaches were designed by Thomas Parker Junior, the GCR carriage & wagon superintendent, and they included both arc-roofed and clerestory stock, the dining cars having raised, American-style clerestories. Automatic couplings were fitted, and the new trains were painted in an attractive two-tone livery, with chocolate below waist level and 'French grey' above. The trains ran in short sets of five or six vehicles. In 1903 the livery was changed to chocolate and cream, though in 1908 the company reverted to a varnished teak colour scheme that recalled earlier Manchester, Sheffield & Lincolnshire practice.

The Parker coaches were later replaced by Robinson stock on the best services but the original London Extension coaches survived for many years on excursions and other less glamorous duties, and they were not finally scrapped until the British Railways period. The later Robinson coaches included a number of distinctive straight-sided vehicles which were built to the maximum width permitted by the Great Central loading gauge.

The goods rolling stock seen at Woodford included large numbers of open wagons for coal and general merchandise traffic. The standard Great Central wagons were unremarkable wooden-bodied vehicles on wooden or steel underframes, many having a capacity of 10 tons. Their livery was grey, with the letters 'GC' displayed in white. In LNER days the Great Central wagon fleet was renumbered in the 500,000 series.

Much of the coal traffic passing through Woodford was carried in privately-owned rolling stock displaying the liveries of numerous collieries or coal merchants, while the connections to the Great Western and Stratford-upon-Avon & Midland Junction systems ensured that 'foreign' rolling stock passed regularly onto the Great Central route.

Some Personal Reminiscences

The men who worked on the Great Central Railway at Woodford during the early years included former construction workers such as William Welch and Harry Gardner, together with established railwaymen who had already started their careers with the Manchester, Sheffield & Lincolnshire Railway. J.H. Peake, for instance, joined the MS&L as a porter in 1889, but transferred to Woodford & Hinton in May 1900. His initial wage was 18s. per week, but on transfer to Woodford he earned 23s. a week as a shunter, with 10d. stopped each week for 'clubs' (i.e. self-help benefit schemes).

Mr Peake was entitled to five days holiday per annum, and he was given one free travel pass by the railway company which could be used only on the Great Central system; many Woodford families used their passes for annual visits to Cleethorpes. After about 46 years service on the railways Mr Peake was given a pension of 2s. 6d. per week, which 'gradually dwindled to nothing at all'! Throughout his working life he had often worked for up to 14 hours a day.

William Welch, who had originally worked for the contractors who built the line, joined the Great Central Railway as a ganger on 1st September, 1899, and worked as a permanent way man for 45 years. Having reached the age of 65, he then worked for a further two years and completed no less than 47 years with the railway company. He moved from Willoughby to Woodford & Hinton shortly after Christmas 1899, and took charge of the permanent way length between Woodford No. 2 Signal Box (then known as Woodford North), northwards towards Charwelton. After a short spell on this length he moved to the 'Station Length', where he remained for the rest of his time on the railway.

One of Mr Welch's duties was the calling out of 'fog men' when they were required for duty, and this entailed a walk to Culworth. On several occasions he got lost in open countryside when trying to take short cuts home across the fields. He got a particular scare one night when he stumbled upon a dark patch of something on the ground in front of him; on touching it with a stick he startled a covey of partridges which noisily burst into the air. He recalled that his hair had stood on end until he realised what had happened!

On another occasion a signalman informed the station master that he wanted the fog men called out and met with the retort, 'Why? I can see the moon plain enough'. The signalman immediately replied, 'We aren't thinking of sending them up there sir!'

A further recollection was of the first aeroplane which flew over Woodford in about 1911. It was following the railway line northwards and the signalmen were able to advise each other from box to box as it passed over. On a footnote, it may be worth mentioning that Mr Welch considered that this pioneer aircraft may have been piloted by Claude Grahame-White (who had purchased an aeroplane from Louis Bleriot and then flown it without instruction). Alternatively, the pilot may have been the colourful Irish-American 'Colonel' S.F. Cody, who had designed and built the British Army's 'Aeroplane No. 1'. It is perhaps more likely, however, that the pilot was Graham Gilmour, who reached 1,200 ft on a flight to Hinton St George before crashing his machine into a fence across a lawn.

Reverting to strictly railway matters, Mr Welch could also remember the south-to-east junction with the East & West Junction Railway being made and subsequently taken out again. The relaying ganger who put it in was called Harry Morritt, and Mr Welch thought that the rails were removed at the east end in about 1911. He could not remember any passenger trains making use of the junction, but he recalled that the signalmen employed at the signal box was named Charity. The desk used in the junction box (which he thought was called Woodford South Box) was begged by Mr Welch for use in his PW cabin near the north Junction at Woodford No. 4 signal box .

Other first-hand recollections of the early days at Woodford & Hinton were provided by Harry Gardner, who joined the GCR as an engine cleaner and became a fireman at, or shortly after, the opening of the line for passenger traffic. He remembered runs to Neasden, via Quainton Road and Harrow, with stops being made at both places for scrutiny by the Railway Clearing House number-takers, together with trips northwards to Annesley. Occasionally, trips were made to West London Junction with trains for the Docks, and on these occasions the route was via Aylesbury, Princes Risborough, High Wycombe and Maidenhead. The enginemen were not allowed to take coal at Neasden unless absolutely necessary.

One of the trains which worked through Woodford & Hinton in the early days was the 2.45 pm London to Milford with all North Eastern traffic, either loaded or empty goods vehicles; a Woodford crew brought the train from London and were relieved there before the northbound working departed at 6.40 pm. The second crew were lodged at Selby. The usual working was two single and two double home trips, which made a week's work.

The first passenger train to run through Woodford recalled by Mr Gardner passed through in 1899, and it was headed by engine No. 89 with driver Ned Grain and fireman Fred France. Engine No. 286 was the first locomotive to work the celebrated 'Newspaper' train from London to Manchester. Mr Gardner remembered that this working was often known as 'The War Express', and no other company was able to convey news of the Boer War to the North in the time allowed.

It is interesting to note that this prestige service was retained after the South African War had ended, and by 1905 the train had become a passenger as well as a newspaper express. Its formation was, however, very light, in part because very few travellers wished to travel north from Marylebone at 2.45 in the morning. The usual load was two bogie passenger coaches, two bogie vans and perhaps five or six four-wheel vans; with such short trains, top link Great Central engines such as the Robinson Atlantics ran through the night at speeds in excess of 80 mph.

The Great Central had an excellent safety record, the one incident recalled by local people being a mishap involving the 6.20 pm express from Marylebone to Bradford on 19th December, 1935. This service was normally an eight-coach formation, but it slipped two vehicles en route, one 'slip' being effected just before Finmere, while the other took place on the approaches to Woodford. On the day in question the Finmere slip was accomplished without any problem but the Woodford slip coach caught up with the main portion of the express and crashed into it after the train had lost speed. Eleven people were injured as a result of the accident.

The practice of slipping vehicles at speed on the Great Central section was ended shortly afterwards, and the 6.20 pm ceased to 'slip' vehicles on 1st February, 1936. This withdrawal meant the end, not only of the Woodford slip coach services, but also of a daily through service between Marylebone and Stratford-upon-Avon that had hitherto been worked to and from Stratford via the link to the former East & West Junction Railway at Woodford West Junction.

A view from the station yard approach road. The large building on the right of Station Road is the White Hart Hotel, built in 1899.   *D. Jackson Collection*

The Gorse Hotel in Hinton was also built in 1899. A small boot and shoe factory owned by the Co-operative Society was once housed in the loft of a former stable at the hotel. This factory employed about 25 local women and girls in the closing room.   *Ruth Irons' Collection*

Chapter Three

A Railway Childhood

When the time came to provide housing for the railway workers, the streets of the old village of Woodford Halse were not even officially named, so the parish council made good the omission. Church Lane became Church Street, and the village church school gave its name to School Street; this led to Scriven's Hill where Miss Pym first established her railwaymen's hostel, and at right angles was High Street. Here was situated my school and on the opposite side of the street, the farrier's workshop run by Tom Ward. This was still operating when I was a child and was a source of great interest to the schoolchildren. Parallel to High Street was South Street with the Fleur-de-lys Public house and Parsons Street, aptly named, for there was the vicarage and the Moravian Church and Manse.

The Railway Village

The contract for building the 200 or so new houses was let to Messrs Melcome Brothers, and the site chosen was on the sloping banks of the River Cherwell. The red bricks used for constructing the houses were made locally at the brickworks just outside the village. The tall chimneys and ruined kilns were still there when I was a child, but were later demolished to make way for new railway sidings.

Incidentally, it was one of the Melcome brothers who obtained a licence to build a kind of hunting lodge at Hinton, opposite the old Manor House. The Gorse, as it was called, was a handsome black and white timbered building with ample stabling for horses at the rear, for the Hunt used to meet often on the green outside. It was a bold venture, but over the years trade declined and the Gorse was bought by the Railway Staff Association as a railwaymen's club. It is still in use as a social club today.

The houses for the railway employees were built in terraces on the grid system. Castle Road, where I was born, and spent my childhood, sloped steeply down to the river, as did its parallel street, Cherwell Terrace. Intersecting them were Percy Road and Sidney Road, named after the contractor's sons, and Church Street merged into Station Road where the shop premises were. There was a long row of shops offering every kind of amenity. They gave to that part of the village an urban appearance, but the sudden increase in population demanded them, and the businesses thrived.

Some of the railway employees were recruited locally, my father for example was a Northamptonshire man, but many of the skilled workers came from further afield. All were eager to take advantage of the new housing, and to seek regular employment with the railway company. There was an astonishing increase in the population from 526 in 1891, to 1,220 in 1901.

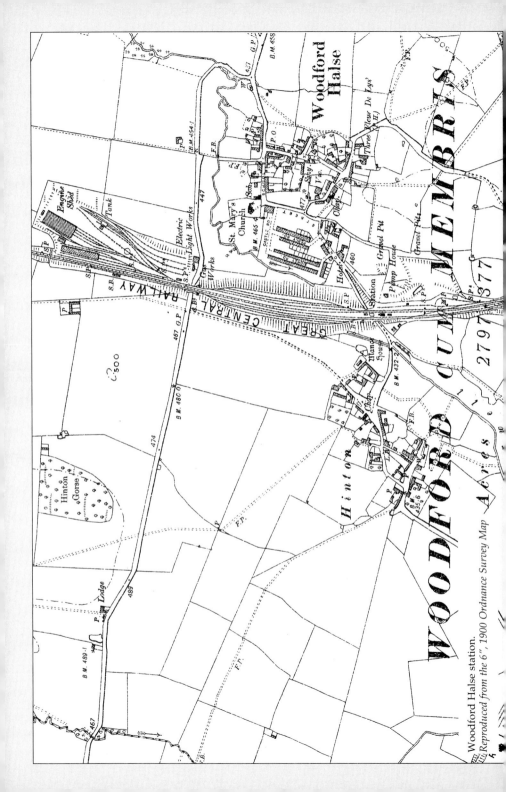

Woodford Halse station.
Reproduced from the 6", 1900 Ordnance Survey Map

Station Road, Woodford Halse.

The row of shops in Station Road which provided us with every amenity. At its northern end, Station Road merged with Church Street, which continued northwards to the parish church.

Ruth Irons' Collection

The gasworks was built about 1909.
Ruth Irons' Collection

Church Street, formerly Church Lane looking south towards Station Road. The opening on the right leads to Castle Road. Aunt and Uncle Needle lived in the house right foreground. *Inset:* Mary, their only child, with my grandfather Knibb who lived with them.

(Both) Ruth Irons' Collection

A later view of Church Street with the Savoy cinema on the right. The first talking films in Woodford were shown here, the earlier Hippodrome being used only for silent films.

Ruth Irons' Collection

A rear view of Sidney Road, Woodford in August 1972.   *D. Jackson Collection*

A view along Sidney Road in August 1972.   *D. Jackson Collection*

Castle Road, Woodford Halse. I was born at No. 19 at the bottom of the picture, but after the age of two, spent my childhood at No. 1 at the top of the hill.   *Ruth Irons' Collection*

Percy Road in 1972. Like Sidney Street, Percy Road was part of the railway village built by Messrs Melcombe Brothers at the end of the 19th century. It ran from north to south on a parallel alignment to Sidney Street. *David Jackson Collection*

A rear view of Sidney Road, my sister was born there. *Ruth Irons' Collection*

A corner of Sidney Road in 1972. Sidney Road and Percy Road were named after the contractor's sons Sidney and Percy Melcombe. No. 69 (*on left*) was for many years the home of Dickie Porter, a driver at Woodford; it is said to have been designed as a public house, although the premises were never used for this purpose. *D. Jackson Collection*

Cherwell Terrace with the former stables on the right. At the time this photograph was taken in 1972, these premises were being used as a shoe factory. *D. Jackson Collection*

Woodford Halse: City of the Future

No better picture of the Woodford existing at the beginning of the century, and of the attitude of the railwaymen can ever be found than that painted by a traveller making his first visit there in March 1903. It is contained in an article he wrote for the local newspaper, the *Daventry Express*, and signed simply, 'A Pilgrim'. It tells how he boarded a train at Marylebone *en route* for Rugby, but at the last moment before the train's departure a telegram was thrust into his hand informing him that his London office required him to break his journey at Woodford & Hinton, a station some 60 miles along the route, there to meet a Mr Dale.

It was a wretched day, and when the traveller arrived at his destination the rain was pouring down, and an icy wind was blowing. He alighted on the platform and wishing to confirm that he had made no mistake, asked a young porter standing nearby if this was indeed Woodford station. 'Yes Sir', was the cheery reply, 'This is Woodford, the City of the Future!' Somewhat irritably the traveller observed that cities take a long time to build, but nothing daunted, the porter replied, 'Yes, but look at the buildings already up!'. The traveller looked, but through the mist of rain saw nothing to justify such faith in Woodford's future greatness. Indeed, he was most reluctant to leave the shelter of the station, but business affairs cannot wait, and he descended the steep wooden steps and made his way to the Post Office, where further instructions awaited him.

The journey was not without mishap. For at one point he slipped on the muddy road and lost, temporarily, his top hat. Furthermore, when he reached the Post Office, a second telegram awaited him with the message that the reason for breaking his journey at Woodford no longer applied, and that there was no need to trouble him further. It was with profound relief that he retraced his steps to the station, later to board a train for Rugby with, as he remarked, ' a feeling of devout pity for the present inhabitants of the City of the Future!'.

It was without doubt, an unfortunate first acquaintance with a railway centre in the making, but the traveller's pity for 'the present inhabitants' was misplaced. There was truly a pioneering spirit aboard in those early days of the railway, and everyone connected with the new enterprise felt proud to be part of it, from the humblest porter upwards.

Family Matters

I was singularly fortunate in my parents. The wages paid by the railway company were small, but my sister and I had a warm, comfortable home, albeit without any of the luxuries considered necessary in ordinary homes today. If, in a material sense, our lives were frugal, in all other essentials we were richly blessed, for we had kind and loving parents. I cherish their memory.

My father, Wilfrid Irons, was born in Daventry on 22nd May, 1887. His father was a bespoke bootmaker, one of many to be found in Northamptonshire in the 19th century. It was almost a home industry, for the

Right: Me, aged 10 months on the chair and sister Margaret 3½ years standing.
Ruth Irons' Collection

Below: A family portrait dating from 1926.
Ruth Irons' Collection

making of boots and shoes was largely carried out by pieceworkers who lived in the town. When, in the 1930s, I taught for four years in a Daventry school, I actually met and talked to an old lady who had once been employed by my grandfather as a pieceworker.

Wilfred, my father, was the youngest of seven children, one of whom died in infancy. The family home was in Abbey Street, but later they moved to premises in High Street which became, after my grandfather's retirement, the retail shop of the boot and shoe firm Stead and Simpson. Both my paternal grandparents died before I was born, but from what I was told, my grandmother was a gentle, ladylike person, much loved by her family. She was the daughter of a farmer in the village of Chipping Warden some three miles as the crow flies from Woodford. The old farmhouse is still there, and the stables where my aunt told me John Wilson, my great grandfather, bred race horses.

My Aunt Margaret was the eldest of the family and the only daughter. She was musical and was well known as a singer, pianist and organist in Daventry. Before her marriage to Frederick York she taught pianoforte, once with commendable enterprise giving free lessons to a pupil in exchange for tuition in the French language. Her son Robert was an incipient railway 'buff' and visited us frequently to spend blissful hours trainspotting on Woodford station.

Uncle John was the only son to carry on his father's trade of selling and repairing boots and shoes. He had a business in the mining area around Swadlincote in Derbyshire and raised five daughters. My sister and I had many happy holidays with them. It was our first taste of life in an industrial society which, compared to that of a railway village, was often marred by real poverty and deprivation.

Father was not the only member of his family to work for a railway company, for his brother Alfred emigrated to South Africa to work in the offices of a company there, and Edwin, another brother, was a railway booking clerk. His death at the age of 23 from tuberculosis persuaded my father that he should seek an outdoor occupation, a wise decision, since some years later another brother, Walter, succumbed to that dreaded disease.

Wilfred, my father, was a remarkable man, who had the circumstances of his life been different, would undoubtedly have become a scholar, like his first cousin from the Wilson family in Birmingham, who was Merton Professor of Literature at Oxford. Wilfred's love of books and learning manifested itself early in life, and he remembered his brief schooldays with gratitude, despite the fact that he suffered many canings for being late for lessons. The excuse that he gave, that he had been on an errand for his father, happened to be true, but it did not save him from punishment. Father regretted all his life that his formal education was of so short a duration, but he did what so many clever men of his generation and in similar circumstances were forced to do, he gained as much knowledge as he could from books.

The small library he inherited from his old home was greatly cherished, and he added to it by buying, through his newspaper, cheap editions of books on a variety of subjects. I have on my bookshelves now, and refer to them often, a set of Encyclopaedia published by Odham's Press in 1933, and I am constantly

My father's family. *Above left:* His sister Margaret Irons, an accomplished musician and teacher. *Above right:* Brother Alfred, who emigrated to South Africa to work in the offices of a railway company there. *Below left:* Brother Edwin, a railway office booking clerk. *Below right:* Brother Walter, an amateur artist.   *(All) Ruth Irons' Collection*

finding between the leaves, small scraps of paper which were his bookmarks. It brings him very near to me. Father enjoyed especially the novels of Charles Dickens, and frequently quoted passages from them. Indeed, he was something of a Dickensian character himself, with a droll sense of humour, and a keen eye for the absurdities of life. He was also a sensitive man and this helped him laugh away the hurts inevitable in the rough and tumble of life in a railway village.

In retrospect, I cannot imagine how my father found time to read at all, for apart from fulfilling admirably his duties as a family man and householder, he gave, in the exercise of his considerable gifts, unstinting service to the people of the village.

My mother, though she supported father in all his activities, was by nature modest and reserved. Her interests were centred primarily on the home, and in providing for her family a warm and comfortable environment. She was born in Charwelton in Northamptonshire, the eldest of four children. Her father, Alfred Knibb, worked on the estate of Sir Charles Knightley at nearby Fawsely, and the family home was a thatched tied cottage within a stone's throw of the parish church. I never knew my maternal grandmother Kezia Knibb, for she died of pneumonia at the early age of 47, but I remember my grandfather as a gentle, rather beautiful old man who patiently taught me to tell the time when I was about six years old.

Mother's sister, Sarah Ann was the one who stayed at home to look after her widowed father, and who after her marriage to George Needle took him to live with them at Woodford. Sally learned to play the piano and violin under the tutelage of a Mr Foorte at Rugby, whose son Reginald Foorte was a popular cinema organist of his day. She became a music teacher like my Aunt Margaret, and taught both my sister and me to play the piano and violin.

Alfred, the third child, grew up to become a railwayman, and made his home at Mexborough in Yorkshire. He and his wife Florence had one daughter, Irene, who came to stay with us often, and dazzled my sister and me with her collection of pretty clothes, all in immaculate condition.

The youngest of the Knibb family, George, enlisted in the Royal Navy, and became our beloved 'Sailor Uncle'. What excitement there was when he came home on leave, bearing gifts from foreign parts! He remained a bachelor until his late forties when he married twice, first to a widow in Leeds, and after her death to Florence, Alfred's widow.

Grandparents, uncles, aunts and cousins, whether alive, or known to me only through accounts given by my family, were very important to me as a child. I loved the feeling of identity within an extended family, and with one notable exception, of whom I shall write more later, my memories of them are of the happiest. Times have changed, but before the advent of the motor car and cheap foreign travel, relations often spent their summer holidays with us, and we returned their visits.

The thatched cottage on the right was my mother's childhood home at Charwelton.

Ruth Irons' Collection

Emma Kezia Knibb (my mother) 1885-1967. This photograph was taken before her marriage in 1910 when she was working in London.

Ruth Irons' Collection

My Aunt Sarah (mother's sister) and her husband George Needle on their wedding day. George later became an engine driver. Sarah taught pianoforte and violin. *Ruth Irons' Collection*

A view of the Barracks from the embankment in 1956.   *D. Jackson Collection*

A fire appliance is in attendance at the scene of a fire at the Barracks on 24th June, 1957.
D. Jackson Collection

Village Life

My parents were married in Charwelton parish church on the 15th October, 1910. I see from their marriage certificate that father, then aged 23, was already a railway fireman, so he must have lived in lodgings at Woodford for a year or so prior to his marriage. The normal progression for a footplate man was from engine cleaner, fireman, and finally driver, but so great was the need for skilled men at that time, that his service as a cleaner was probably of short duration.

My parents' first home was a rented, three-storied house at No. 54, Sidney Road. Because of the sloping ground on the banks of the River Cherwell, the house was built on two levels. The front entrance was from the street, while from the rear, access was through a large cellar kitchen. It was said that the mother of one young railwayman, a motor bike enthusiast, always had the door of her kitchen wide open when her son returned from work, so that he could drive straight in, to the storeroom beyond!

It was in just such a kitchen, years later, that I watched with the utmost fascination, an old lady mulling her stout. She heated a poker in the grate and when it was red-hot, plunged it into a mug of stout. There was a loud sizzling sound, and I remember marvelling how anyone could drink such a dangerous concoction.

In the same road was the railway hostel, always known as 'The Barracks' where single railwaymen were given accommodation, and later, 'foreign crews' operating from further afield could lodge for the night.

From a housewife's point of view, No. 54 was a most inconvenient house to manage, and after the difficult birth of my sister Margaret in 1913, the family moved to a house at No. 19 Castle Road, where on 23rd April, 1917, I made my entry into the world. It was a miracle that I survived at all. My mother told me that the first words she heard from the doctor who delivered me were, 'It's a fine girl, but oh my God, look at her neck!'. Indeed, I had a large swelling on the right side of my neck which impeded my breathing, and threatened to suffocate me. The local Vicar was hastily summoned, and I was christened there and then in the bedroom. Years after, the then vicar of the parish showed me the entry of my birth in the parish register, with the word 'Private' against the record of my baptism.

My dear father was the only one who had faith in my survival. He did all he could, and took me to be examined by an Ear, Nose and Throat Specialist in Birmingham who pronounced that I was too young for an operation, and gave me a 50/50 chance of survival. But survive I did, the swelling subsided, and I grew into a plump, healthy child. When I was about 2 years-old, my father had a small legacy from his brother Walter, and for the first time became a proud house-owner. We moved to a house higher up the road at No. 1 vacated by my mother's sister Sarah and her husband George Needle, who moved to Church Street. The house was vastly superior to the other homes in that it had the luxury of a bathroom. Water was heated in the kitchen copper and conveyed upstairs to the bathroom by a rotary pump, which seemed to us a step up in the world from our former method of using a tin bath in the kitchen.

Driver Walt Pratt and fireman Reg Langston look down from the footplate of Thompson 'B1' class 4-6-0 No. 1123.   *Ruth Irons' Collection*

Uncle George was something of a handyman, and he bequeathed to us a rather beautiful dark green marble fireplace which he had installed in the living room, and I do not think it ever occurred to us how incongruous a fixture it was in such a setting. In the bow-windowed front sitting room facing the street was kept our upright rosewood piano with the name 'Reginald Foorte' in gold letters on the inside of the lid, so it must have come from the Rugby shop of my Aunt's music teacher. On a stand in the corner of the room was my mother's prized possession, an aspidistra plant, without which, in those days, no parlour was considered complete. There were three bedrooms, and since from the rear of the house we over-looked the old Norman church and graveyard, the back bedroom afforded us a splendid view of weddings and funerals.

Always, through nearly every hour of the day or night, there was the clamour of the railway. The noise of hissing steam from engines, the clanging and crashing of shunting wagons, and the thunder of express trains as they flew along the high embankment near my home were entirely natural to me as a child. Only when we stayed in a place, with relations perhaps, where such sounds were absent, did we miss the sound of that busy traffic, and then we felt very strange indeed because of the uncanny quiet. On the contrary, visitors who stayed with us expressed surprise that we could sleep so soundly amidst such clamour.

Housewives were so familiar with the times of the trains that they set their clocks by them. When the express train from the South, 'The Bournemouth' came through, they knew that their children would soon be returning from school and it was time to prepare tea. To hear the 'Fish Train' speeding along the embankment about 11.30 pm, carrying its load from Grimsby and the North-East meant that after retiring to bed, sleep was slow in coming, and those who craved real sympathy had merely to state, 'I never closed my eyes until the Mail came through!' When trains were late, they knew about it, and there was sometimes a feeling of disquiet when the men's return home from duty was for long delayed.

Much is heard today about labour which involves 'unsocial hours' and rightly, some compensation is demanded for those who work while others sleep. By this precept, footplate men should have been rich indeed. In my childhood, when someone asked me the simple question, 'Is your father at home?', I was often hard put to give the correct reply. Frequently, he would be in bed during daylight hours, enjoying a well earned rest after working a nightshift, but the changes in hours of duty were bewildering for a child. One thing we learnt at an early age was that our father's rest time was sacred. At such times it was not allowed to burst exuberantly into the house, play noisy games indoors, or practise on the piano. It was not quite such an embargo as that imposed on his family by the somewhat autocratic father of my sister's friend, who when he was sleeping upstairs, met my sister at the door with fingers on lips, and conducted all conversation in whispers.

The normal hours of work for footplate men was in 8-hour shifts from 6 am onwards. Overtime was paid for work done over this period and the rosters never extended beyond nine hours. For men working the midnight to 6 am shift a 'knocker-up' was employed to make sure that the men arrived for duty on time. Often I have heard in the early hours of the morning his knock on the front door, and his voice saying, 'Will, time for duty!'. The story is told how one 'knocker-up' became so exasperated by receiving no response to his call that he stationed himself on the opposite side of the road to the house in question, and took a running jump at the front door, thereby sustaining some injury to his toes in the process, and doubtless also to the painted door.

I attribute my mother's ability to wake at any hour of the night or early morning on demand, to my father's hours of work, and I always marvelled at her 'mental alarm clock' which enabled her to do this. When he went on duty, father took with him a tin box with his name in brass on the lid. This contained a snack, and in a separate compartment his Book of Rules without which no footplate man was ready for duty. Before facilities were provided for 'brewing up' he also had an enamel can for a cold drink, and in wartime a hand lamp fed with paraffin.

It was necessary for a footplate man to arrive at the locomotive department one hour before duties actually began. Diagrams and notices were posted there and these had to be studied for the necessary information about the duties for the shift. Then the locomotive had to be examined and made ready for operation. This involved oiling it and checking that the coal supply was in order.

There were varied duties. Men on the 'Shed Shunt' had to ensure that the engine was in the right order for leaving the shed to collect the wagons and sometimes an engine had to be shunted into a siding until it was needed. Passenger crews had to learn the location of the carriages and collect them ready for their journeys.

It was indeed a highly organised system which enabled the trains to run according to schedule, and this was but part of the enterprise. Platelayers, fitters, repair and wagon shop workers, signalmen and station staff all played their part, to mention but a few of the workers involved. It was truly a communal enterprise, and in the early days of the railway at Woodford, everyone felt it to be so, and took a real interest in the work.

There were accidents of course, and errors were made. A grim reminder of the hazards which lay ahead for railwaymen is the tombstone in Woodford churchyard commemorating the death in 1864 of William Davis aged 22 years, who had left the village in the early days of the railways to work in Camden Town. He was killed by an explosion of an engine boiler. Years later, a similar accident happened to the fireman of a Woodford driver, Stan Yates, when there was a blow-back from the engine which caused the fireman severe burns and resulted in his death later in hospital. On the same day, it is recorded that E. Kite was knocked down by a light engine and suffered serve head injuries.

Sometimes, of course, fatal accidents were caused by men growing careless through the familiarity of walking and working along the lines. I will never forget the day when my father, the kindest and gentlest of men came home from work to tell us that he had killed a workman while shunting his engine up at the sheds. It was, I remember, a Friday, and the thirteenth of the month, and though we were not, on the whole, a superstitious family, the date of the accident was firmly imprinted on my mind. My father, courageous as always, talked of the incident in matter of fact terms, but we were not fooled by his apparent calm, for it was a terrible experience for him, and later in the day I came upon him sitting with his head in his hands in a rare attitude of grief and despondency. No blame was attached to father over the accident. It was the old story - a railwayman's familiarity with those iron monsters breeding carelessness in walking along the track.

A Law Abiding Community

It was a plus factor in our newly-formed community that we were hardly ever haunted by the spectre of unemployment. Pupils leaving school at 14 soon found work. Sons of farmers went on the land, and because of easy access by rail to the neighbouring towns, others found work in offices, shops and factories. Boys who wished to follow their fathers as railway employees could, when the vacancies arose, serve as apprentices in the wagon shops, or join the station staff, but those who yearned to be engine drivers had to wait until they were 16 to begin the long apprenticeship for so responsible a job.

My father, in his turn, was one of the experienced drivers who helped to train the young firemen to achieve this ambition. The Improvement Class, as it was called, used to meet in a disused railway carriage in the goods yard. Incidentally, when, during my teens, the parish council bought land for a playing field, and a tennis club was formed, an old railway carriage provided an excellent vehicle for refreshments at tournaments and tennis matches against visiting teams.

We were, on the whole, a law abiding community. One rule was established very early for the children of railwaymen. Never, never, must we trespass on railway property; it was for our own safety of course, but I always felt that there was an underlying threat to our father's employment if we transgressed in that direction. Actually, I think it remarkable that in all my childhood there was never one case of vandalism, injury or death to children through trespassing on the railway line. This is remarkable in view of the fact that the main line passed right through the centre of the village, and alongside the meadows where we played. I do not suppose that the young boys of the village were entirely blameless. We did know of one small gang who used to go up to the old brickyard to put pennies on the railway line, to be retrieved in their flattened state after the express trains stopped there to take water from the pumps. We were very shocked when we heard of such daring deeds.

Law abiding as we were, my friends from the High School and I once did a very reprehensible thing. In an excess of joy at the end of one summer term, we tore up our season tickets into small fragments. The expression of amazement on the ticket collector's face as we handed the pieces to him, seemed hilarious at the time. There were repercussions of course, severe reprimands from our fathers, one of whom happened to be the station master. We were made to feel that though we were, one and all, guilty of a crime against the company, the station master's daughter had really let the side down!

As for the adults, though there were four public houses in the village, and each had their habitués, drunkenness was fairly rare. We viewed those who frequented the public houses rather pityingly, for my father abhorred strong drink, and strict non-conformists as we were, the public houses were thought of as rather sinful places.

Strangely enough, though father drank neither wine nor spirits, an exception was made in the case of homemade wine, which was really rather potent, and was served sparingly in whiskey glasses. Only once did I ever see a member of my family in a state of intoxication after drinking home-made wine. It happened, unbelievably, to my dear devout old grandfather who lived with an aunt in the village. One day while we were sitting in her kitchen, grandfather came in exhausted after an excessive stint of gardening, and my aunt, thinking to revive him, administered not one but two glasses of her parsnip wine. Not long afterwards, my sister and I sat open-mouthed as grandfather's voice rose at least two octaves, and his mumbled sentences were interspersed with cackles of laughter. It was a salutary experience for both of us.

Many of the railwaymen's wives made wine, for the main ingredients were ready to hand. My sister and I enjoyed our excursions in search of the golden heads of dandelions, and the beautiful burnet that grew in the meadows along the Preston Road. Potatoes, parsnips, rhubarb, and different fruits were all used in their turn, and in the summer, mother used to make for us delicious elderflower champagne. I can see their creamy heads now, floating in the large stone jars in the larder. The champagne was non-alcoholic of course, and its season was short-lived, because of its speedy fermentation and the danger of exploding bottles.

Looking back over the years, I think there was a kind of happy innocence about all my childish experiences, and a feeling of total security in that close-knit community, which enabled us to wander for miles about the country lanes without fear of molestation, and though at night there were always men going to work, mugging and robbery were unknown. Human nature does not change, but the framework in which we live our lives has changed. There was a moral discipline about that hard-working society which mitigated against the worst excesses of which human nature is capable.

Social Behaviour

In a small, close knit community, where most of the railwaymen and their families lived in terrace houses in close proximity to neighbours, the family unit was very important. Most housewives took a fierce pride in keeping up appearances, and seeing that their homes were clean and that their children went to school decently clad and knew how to behave themselves in adult company. Such aims were not achieved without sacrifices and hard work for the life of a railwayman's wife was by no means an easy one.

For men on shift work meals had to be provided at irregular hours and sleep was disturbed when the 'knocker-up' called men away for duty. The maintenance and operation of those giant machines was dirty work and overalls soon became soiled with oil, grease and coal dust. Before the days of washing machines, these had to be scrubbed manually and it was particularly hard work for wives who had more than one railwayman in the family.

My mother was an excellent cook, with a specially light hand in making pastry. In my early days all the cooking was done on a coal-fired iron stove in the kitchen, and it was a point of honour with her, as with many wives, to keep this primitive apparatus scoured and polished. She was also well acquainted with the activity 'make do and mend' a phrase coined during the World War II, but practised by her from the beginning of her married life. Yet despite all the shifts necessary to keep a respectable home, I recognise in retrospect that she had a touching longing for beautiful things, for from her small housekeeping allowance she would save for months, even years, to buy some small article of furniture that she set her heart on. There was a delicate mahogany tub chair I remember, with a blue silk seat, and an oval inlaid mirror, both of which graced our front room.

My mother was generous to a fault, and the only cause of dissension between her and my father was when she overspent the house-keeping money. I have often wondered if father had some premonition that he would not live to see old age, for he was always extremely careful with money, in order, he said, that if anything happened to him, my mother would not have to go out to work to support the family. And indeed, though his estate when he died would seem negligible by today's standards, his savings did represent careful planning and wise investments, sometimes, with commendable enterprise, in stocks and shares. It was a mark of the more thrifty railwaymen that they were able, like my father to own their own home, either on the estate, or in one of the new houses springing up on the outskirts of the village.

But for me, as a child, our house in Castle Road was perfect in every way, warm and secure, with a mother who was always there to minister to our needs. I liked the feeling of being in the centre of things with school, shops, and friends within easy reach. Our relations with our neighbours were always cordial, though mother was a rather private person who never indulged in the habit of popping into someone's house uninvited for a cup of tea and a gossip.

It was different with my aunt and uncle who lived in Church Street, a stone's throw away, for they were family, and with them our relations were very close indeed. We loved dearly my aunt, mother's sister, and grandfather Knibb who lived with her, but Uncle George was an unpredictable man, and we never knew in what mood we should find him. He was a railwayman like my father, and was a tall, burly figure who in his prime possessed great physical strength. His skill, as I shall recount later, in doing household repairs and plumbing made him a very useful member of the community, and he was in great demand.

In contrast to his less endearing traits of character, he had great love for flowers and was an expert gardener, an inheritance from his aged parents who still lived in the village, and from whom one could buy for a few pence, a bunch of the loveliest cottage flowers. In his greenhouse Uncle grew beautiful orchids and other exotic plants, purely for his own pleasure and pride, for I do not believe that he ever exhibited them at the local flower shows. And on special occasions when relatives were visiting, or on Christmas Day when we were always invited for tea, he could be a most genial host. I can see him now as he presided benignly over a table laden with delicious food prepared by my aunt, and with their beautiful Crown Derby tea set on display. How much, even as a small child, I envied them that elegant china!

Yet at other times, and frequently, he would be moody and difficult, consumed with anger against some imagined wrong. Not even my good father escaped his censure, and I found it incomprehensible that open enmity should sometimes erupt against someone held in such high esteem in the community. The kindness and patience with which my parents dealt with this difficult relative, and the support they gave to my aunt through all the years of her married life, were exemplary. When their only child, my cousin Mary, contracted meningitis at the age of eleven, it was mother who helped my aunt nurse the child through that last fatal illness, and when, soon after Uncle's health began to fail, it was to my father that he turned for comfort and practical medical help.

Strangely, I do not believe that anyone in the community ever knew of the difficulties my parents suffered by Uncle's behaviour. It was a family affair, and my parents would have thought it to be beneath their dignity to make public such intimate troubles. I am sure that for many of the railwaymen's families this code applied, for it was a matter of pride to most of them to keep the good name of the family intact.

My sister and I were strictly trained in correct social behaviour. We were taught from an early age to show due respect to all adults, to respond politely to greetings, to refrain from interrupting adult conversation, and to behave in a disciplined manner in company. I am sure that my sister never once transgressed in this respect, but the two occasions in, my early childhood when 'I let the side down' remain very vividly in my memory. One occurred when I was out walking with my father and we met a fellow railwayman. As always when two of the fraternity got together, the talk was of work. I must have been overcome by resentment at being excluded from the conversation, for I suddenly, with legs firmly astride, protruded my infant stomach, patted it, and announced loudly, 'I am Fatty Arbuckle!' (Fatty Arbuckle was a popular comedian of the day.) I can see now the flush which suffused father's face, and the steely look in his grey eyes. I knew at once that I had 'over stepped the mark' and the experiment in attention seeking was never repeated.

I transgressed a second time when a friend of my mother came to take afternoon tea with us. The lady in question and her husband Jack were childless. Their home was immaculate and there were frequent changes in the furnishings. Mother, I remember, bought second-hand from them a brown velvet three piece suite which graced our sitting room for years. As so often happens with childless couples, husband and wife were very close entwined, and throughout the tea party it was Jack this, and Jack that, until my infant patience was exhausted. So when at last the husband came to the door to collect his wife, I piped up in resigned tones, 'Here's Jack!'. There was a horrified silence, and once again I was made aware of the enormity of my offence. For a child to use an adult's Christian name without the honorary title of Aunt or Uncle, was entirely out of order.

Times have changed, but I think the precepts laid down by my parents in the matter of social behaviour and the need for courtesy and consideration in dealings between children and adults is a good basis for a decent society, of whatever class. Because ours was such a close-knit community, family loyalty was necessary if privacy was to be maintained and to this day, and throughout our long lives, my sister and I always been reticent to broadcast, outside the family circle, the disappointments and griefs that come to all of us at some time in our personal lives.

Medical Services

We had two doctors who served the people of the parish. Dr Hope lived at nearby Byfield and Dr Glencose Hays was resident in Woodford Halse at Jaffa House, one of the older stone-built and thatched buildings in the village. We were very much in awe of Dr Hays who attended to our family's medical needs. He was a short, gruff, cigar-smoking man with a drooping nicotine-stained moustache, and he did not suffer malingerers lightly. I have vivid memories of sitting in the patients' waiting room at Jaffa House, which must have been a converted out-house. The walls of brick, painted over, dripped with moisture, and a wag once remarked that if one was not ill before visiting the surgery, there was a grave danger of contracting a severe cold through sitting in that extremely damp room.

From the adjoining surgery the doctor dispensed his simple remedies, never, so far as I can remember, in tablet form. The dispensing of bottled medicines presented some problems in the early days when Woodford had its own water supply, conveyed by gravity from a tank at the top of Fox Hill. Jaffa House was the highest point in the supply area, and there was frequently a shortage of water. It was said that on such occasions. the Doctor put the necessary medicines in the bottle with strict instructions to the patient to add water when arriving home. Later, in 1936, when a reservoir was constructed on the Daventry Road, Woodford's water supply became adequate for the increased demand, but the reservoir at the top of Fox Hill was still there when I was young. The old padlocked door that gave access to the tank below held a frightening fascination for us children, for through the wooden slats there was a glimpse of the water below, dark and mysterious.

In retrospect, medical care in the early days of the railway does seem to have been rather primitive, for though hospital treatment for railwaymen and their families was available, a curious system existed by which a 'Letter of Introduction' had to be obtained before treatment could be given. The letters were in the hands of local subscribers to the voluntary hospitals usually members of the gentry or clergymen. Not surprisingly, there was an objection by the more radical members of the railwaymen who hated to take part in a process which smacked of charity, and when it was found that the 'Letters of Introduction' could be purchased, steps were taken to raise funds to buy them. A Hospital Sunday Committee was formed, and from 13th April, 1924 27 events were organised for this purpose. Collections were taken at the local churches, and proceeds from dances and concerts helped to swell the funds. Best of all, for me, and for all the village children, was the annual Hospital Sunday event held in the Parson's Close in Church Street.

It was a special occasion because on every other day of the year, the Close was forbidden territory. On it grew magnificent sweet and horse chestnut trees. I do not think that my sister and I, law-abiding as we were, ever climbed the stone wall surrounding the Close to gather the sweet nuts or conkers, but braver souls often trespassed and ran the risk of incurring the wrath of Parson Smith who lived in the vicarage on the far side of the Close. So that as we stood under the trees on Hospital Sunday, listening to the brass band belting out the accompaniment to the hymns we sang so lustily, there was a delicious feeling that we were indeed privileged to stand on that sacred ground.

After 1927 the railwaymen decided that this somewhat haphazard method of raising money for the hospital treatment should give way to a more organised procedure. A ballot was taken and 'The Woodford Workers Hospital Fund' came into being. One penny in the pound was contributed from all those who wished to take part in the scheme, and this continued until the National Health Service was put into operation in 1948. When the old fund was wound up in 1948, there was a balance of £233 6s., and a nice touch I think, the money was given to the Hospital of St Cross at Rugby.

The Rugby hospital was the one widely used by Woodford patients, but occasionally they chose to go to the Northampton General Hospital. It was there soon after the World War I that my father had his first and only experience of hospitalisation. He had an operation there for hernia and was deeply offended when a jingoistic Sister accompanying the doctors on their round of the ward, stopped at the foot of his bed and said, 'You did not, I believe, Irons, serve your King and Country in the Forces!' I can well imagine the quiet dignity with which he made his reply, 'No, I served my Country in other ways'. He spoke truly, for the lives of railwaymen during wartime was hard and often dangerous. They worked long hours transporting men and supplies, and made a notable contribution to the war effort.

I am somewhat puzzled to know why my father chose to have his operation at the Northampton hospital, for there was direct access to Rugby on the Great Central Line, whereas the train journey to Northampton meant a walk of two miles to the village of Byfield in order to catch a train on the old LMS line. I do know, because he often mentioned his ordeal, that when he was discharged from the Northampton Hospital he had to *walk* the two miles from Byfield to Woodford. He was so weak after the operation that he had to rest several times by the road side before finally reaching home. In the days before the Ambulance Service, and the availability of taxis and private cars, the problem of getting to and from hospital for those early railwaymen and their families, was inconceivably difficult.

It would have been interesting if, during the first half century in the history of the railway at Woodford, a survey could have been instituted to gauge the effect of their work on the health and longevity of the men who operated those giant machines. Irregular hours of employment, extremes of temperature from the heat of the furnace, and cold from the open-sided cab, together with the jolting and shaking of the engine travelling at speed, all these factors must have taken their toll. Indeed, as I look back it seems to me that the number of men who lived many years past retirement age, was very small indeed.

In later years I never, alas, had the opportunity to observe at close quarters how an engineman adjusted from that busy communal life to one of leisure and retirement. My father died when he was 59 years of age, and in any case he was by then no longer an engine driver, but had been promoted to 'Acting Oil Inspector', a post which had its stresses and difficulties, for in that sturdy, independent community, some men did not take kindly to receiving directions from someone 'risen from the ranks', however well the promotion may have been merited.

This I know, and it has always been a source of regret to me, that father did not to live to enjoy a few peaceful years at the end of his working life. How he would have revelled in leisure for reading and study, for tending his garden, and while strength lasted to continue with his contributions to the life of the village! Imagine, he might even have been one of that small group of ex-drivers who during the summer months used, in the course of their walks along the country lanes, to find some convenient place where they could rest and discuss some book or other, usually supplied by my father. A favourite was his prized *History of Northamptonshire* issued in 1849 by William Whellan and Co., I have it still.

My memory may be at fault, but it does seem to me that in contrast to the elderly men of the village, there were many more women who lived to old age. Many of them were widows, and some still wore the long skirts of the Edwardian period. The lady who lived in Sidney Road and afforded me so much interest by mulling her stout, was such a one. She often visited my mother, and I do not think that the occasions were entirely uplifting ones, for the visitations always ended in tears, as the old lady mourned afresh the loss of her railwayman husband, long since deceased. The congregation at our church had a fair share of elderly widows, and truth to tell, I found them rather intimidating, for they did not take kindly to childish high spirits.

The St John Ambulance Brigade

No record of the medical care and treatment available to the railwaymen and their families in those early days would be complete without some reference to the valuable work done by members of the St John Ambulance Brigade. The movement in Woodford was very strong. Minor accidents and some major ones were not uncommon with railway work and in such cases a man skilled in first aid was invaluable.

Father joined the brigade early in his career, for he was very interested in, and read widely on the function of the human body and the cause and treatment of its ills. Indeed, had the opportunity been given him, he would have made an excellent doctor. I can see his hands now, the fingers strong and practical - healing hands, for he learned the art of massage, and could soothe away many an ache and pain.

Above: The Woodford Ambulance
Team with the coveted Maclure
Cup which they won in
competition with teams from other
depots in 1919.
                  Ruth Irons' Collection

The Manor House at Hinton was occupied during medieval times by the De Hinton family who took
their name from the hamlet. Successive owners included, during the 17th century, the Spencers of
Althorp, and later, a branch of the Knightleys of Fawsely. During my childhood, a farmer, Mr George
Phipps, lived there and the gardens where opened annually for social events organised by the St John's
Ambulance Brigade.   *Ruth Irons' Collection*

The small group of railwaymen who were keen on learning about first aid and home nursing met regularly to practise their skills. Sometimes Dr Hope came over from Byfield to lecture on various subjects, but at other times father and one or two men, senior members of the group, acted as lay instructors. The Woodford Locomotive Ambulance team did well in competition with teams from other railway depots, and in 1913, and again in 1919, won the much coveted Maclure Cup. From time to time, grateful members of the Brigade presented father with gifts to mark their appreciation of his untiring service in the cause; one of them, a handsome barometer, now hangs on the wall of our cottage.

I have before me now on my desk, his silver watch chain. Apart from the links at the end to which was attached his fob watch, it is made up of dated silver bars awarded each year to those who successfully passed the First Aid and Home Nursing examinations. The links begin in 1912 and continue until 1941. Also in my possession are gold bars awarded for 10, 15, and 30 years. And there was the never to be forgotten day on 20th December, 1936, when my mother, resplendent in a new hat, accompanied my father to London to receive at the hands of Arthur, Duke of Connaught and Strathearn, Grand Prior of the Order, the medal of Serving Brother in, as the handsome certificate records, the first year of His Majesty's reign. Since this must refer to Edward the VIII whose reign ended one month later, the certificate has historic interest.

An abiding memory of my childhood is of the many occasions, at all hours of the day and night, when there would be a knock on our door, and an anxious voice saying, 'Could Mr Irons come please, we need help'. In truth, he was a kind of unofficial doctor to the village. It went beyond his competence in dressing wounds, bandaging sprains and even setting broken limbs - people had confidence in him and sought his advice in many aspects of health care.

Whenever he could be of service, he was always willing to respond to any call for help, however unpleasant the task before him. When, for instance, there was a terrible accident at the Sheds and an engine ran over a railwayman, severing both his legs. Somehow, with tourniquets I suppose, he managed to keep the man alive until he could be taken to hospital. The unfortunate victim of this accident did not survive, but the railway company recognised my father's attempt to keep the man alive, and awarded him a medal for first aid rendered at Woodford, 10th August, 1923.

The medal awarded to father by the railway company. The reverse has this inscription 'Awarded to W. Irons for First Aid rendered at Woodford. August 10th, 1923'.

Ruth Irons' Collection

The last photograph of my father, taken in the garden of my Birmingham home, shortly before his death in 1946.   *Ruth Irons' Collection*

An inquest was held at Rugby shortly afterwards, and it transpired that the unfortunate victim had been suffering from headaches and insomnia. His brother had recently died, and this had upset him considerably, while on the morning of the tragedy he had told his wife that he was feeling unwell; before leaving for work the deceased and gone out into the garden and picked a single flower which he had given to her. A short time later James Smith, a signalman, was leaning out of the window of his cabin when he saw a man running across the rails into the path of a train. The Jury decided that the deceased man had died of shock after throwing himself under a train whilst of unsound mind, and expressed sympathy for the widow; the Coroner commended the railway ambulance men and said that the railway company should be glad to have such men at Woodford.

There were so many incidents during my father's lifetime that common sense, prompt action and his skill in first aid helped him to avert suffering amongst people who came to him for help. One such incident was not told to me until many years after it occurred, because of the secrecy involved. Father was called out one night by the family of a woman who, overcome by the sorrows of life, had attempted to take her life by gassing herself. In those less compassionate days, it was an offence against the law to attempt suicide, so after father had successfully resuscitated her, everyone concerned was sworn to secrecy. If I know my father, the affair would not have ended there, and he would have used his skill as a wise counsellor to help the unfortunate woman and her family to overcome their difficulties. Indeed the woman survived for some years, and the suicide attempt was never repeated.

Sometimes I bathed in reflected glory from my father's expertise in rendering first aid, when, for instance he came to visit the headmaster of the village school where I was a pupil, and a child fell in the playground and broke a limb, and father set the fracture so skilfully that he was congratulated by the hospital on his efficiency. I remember too, how when there was an accident at the bottom of our road, I was dispatched to bring first aid equipment from our house, and ran with eager feet up and down the street, full of childish importance. But there was one occasion when my heart failed me, and I removed myself from the scene. It happened one evening when our burly Scout master appeared at the door with a child in his arms. Protruding from the child's knee was an enormous darning needle. I fled, and how my father dealt with the situation I never knew.

The final and most touching tribute to father's work came in 1946 when he died suddenly while gardening on the acre of land he and my brother-in-law had purchased on the outskirts of the village. When his body was brought home to our house in Castle Road, a deputation of men from the brigade came to ask mother if they could perform the last rites of preparing his body for burial. I shall never forget how my poor mother wept bitterly because in the stress of the moment, she inadvertently gave them with his burial garments, a pair of socks with a small darn in the heel. It was the same men who proudly bore his coffin to the last resting place, a fitting climax to a life of service in the cause, best summed up in a letter mother received after his death, written by a neighbour who found his body. My mother had written to him to thank him for summoning help by calling the doctor, though it was already too late to save father's life. Our neighbour's reply was thus, 'I was glad to do what little I could, to help someone who all his life did all that *he* could to help his fellow men - myself included, *Which can never be repaid!*'

School Street. The Church of England school is on the left of the photograph. Woodford's
Manor House is the tall building on the left.   *Ruth Irons' Collection*

The council school Woodford Halse. I was a pupil there from 1921 until 1928. Many of the
railway families sent their children to this school, whereas the long-established agricultural
families preferred the Church school. There was thus a religious distinction between the two
schools, the council school being dominated by non-conformist children. *Ruth Irons' Collection*

Chapter Four

Life in Woodford
Education, Religion and Entertainment

A village community takes years to come into being, but remarkably, by the time I was born, and so soon after the sudden influx of population, it was already taking shape. I have written at length of the provisions made for the physical well being of the inhabitants, but there were other needs to be met in the schools, churches and places of entertainment.

The Village Schools

Perhaps the village schools (and there were two) pinpoint the dual elements in village life the old and the new. The Church School, endowed by Sir Henry Dryden of Canons Ashby, had been begun in 1856. When he failed to get the local landowners to contribute towards its cost Sir Henry, at his own cost, had the walls constructed to a height of six feet with a roof of thatch, and it was not until 1867 that the building was handed over to the Vicar and churchwardens. I little thought when I was a child that one day I would spend nine happy years as a teacher in that same building. My classroom window commanded a view of the old Norman church and graveyard, and I remember how, in the early spring sunshine, cats would sun themselves on the flat tombstones.

The original school, with its three classrooms, soon became inadequate to house the large number of children from the railwaymen's families, and new classrooms were therefore built on the same site. Then in 1912 a fine new council school was constructed in the High Street. It seemed to the people of Woodford that here was progress at last, for fronting the road there was a large domestic science and craft room, with three good-sized classrooms behind, and beyond the asphalt playground there was a large school garden where the older boys under the supervision of the headmaster grew flowers, fruit and vegetables.

My sister and I attended this school, as did the majority of the railwaymen's children. Truth to tell, it was thought by many of us that the old Church School with its pupils drawn mainly from the farming classes and old established families was no match for the new modern school with its clever and ambitious headmaster, Mr George Cobley.

Because of my habit of wandering abroad, my parents sent me to school when I was barely four years old. Everything about that infants class filled me with delight - the coloured chalks we used for drawing on our small blackboards, the cowry shells with which we made shapes on sand trays, the brightly-coloured beads we threaded on laces in the number lessons, and best of all, the bold black print of our Blackie Readers, with the diphthongs printed in red. I felt completely happy and secure, for my sister Margaret was a pupil at the same school, albeit in a higher class being three years older. She watched over me with tender care, as she has done all her life. One precious memory I have of her from my time in the infants' class, which has been with me through all our years of growing old together, is of an occasion when we were going to stay with relatives and had permission to leave school early. Margaret came to fetch me from the classroom and I can see her now framed in the doorway, in a primrose-coloured dress with her small face alight with excitement, beneath a halo of curls. Little wonder that the teacher exclaimed, 'Why, she's just like a fairy child!'.

My enchantment with school lasted well into the junior class. I was a placid child, much given to day-dreaming, indeed I think I dwelt too much in the world of my imagination. At about the age of nine I was an avid reader, even attempting some writing on my own behalf, mostly in the realm of verse. My old junior teacher, then in her eighties, once told me that she still had a copy of some verses I wrote while I was a pupil in her class. They were, as I remember, about a dying mother's exhortation to her child to live a goodly and righteous life when she was no more! It was this same teacher who gave my friend Edith and me a rare treat. As a reward for doing well in the end of term tests we were invited to her lodgings in the village for afternoon tea in the garden.

Had I but known it such simple pleasures, and the unadulterated enjoyment of school life were coming to a close, for with my elevation to the top class under the headmaster came the awakening knowledge that life was real and earnest and not to be passed in a haze of romantic imaginings. It was in the algebra lessons that I met my Waterloo, for I could not, at first, grasp the principles that governed this somewhat tricky subject. After failing to complete some simple exercise, Mr Cobley, never one to suffer fools gladly, lost his temper with me and as a punishment I was demoted for the morning back to the junior class. I have never forgotten the humiliation I felt as I presented myself, tearfully, to my former teacher. About this time too, I had another hard lesson to learn, for I was subjected to a certain amount of bullying from a fellow pupil. Coming as I did from a loving and protective home, it was a tremendous shock especially as the malice that prompted it was aimed not only at me, but at my family.

Let me explain. My father, son of a master bootmaker, had absorbed many of the skills of not only making, but repairing boots and shoes, as he watched his father's employees at work in his early years. Moreover, when my grandfather's business closed, father inherited some of his tools, and what was more natural than that he should use his skills to keep the family's footwear in good repair. It did not end there, for when neighbours and friends learned of his prowess, they too brought their boots and shoes to be repaired. It was an innocent enough occupation for his spare time, and brought into the family exchequer a few welcome shillings. It was not at all unusual for the railwaymen to use such skills as they possessed to augment their small wages, and their wives often took in lodgers, single men who found employment with the company. My Uncle George Needle was in great demand for he was adept at small building and plumbing repairs.

Father did his shoe repairing in a small lean-to building at the back of the house. In one corner was our coal supply, and on the shelves in front of the small window he kept his leathers and tools, with tucked away at the back, his fishing rods and a pair of ice skates. One severe winter I was immensely proud of my father when he donned his skates and sped over the ice on nearby Byfield Pools, for he was, in his boyhood, a keen skater. Father bought his leather from a store in Leicester and the family outing to purchase it is one of the abiding memories of my childhood. The hides were hung from the ceiling of the shop, and my father would take a long time to choose what he needed for his repairs. The smell of the leather must have been for him a pleasant reminder of the days when he wandered in and out of his father's workshop. Sometimes the kind manager gave my sister and me some brightly coloured advertising cards to take home, and after we left the shop we would go to Leicester Market to buy some fish for tea. Then there was the journey home, when space permitting, Margaret and I would curl up on the railway carriage's plush seats and lulled by the sound of the wheels going over the points and jointed track, would rest quietly until the train entered the Catesby Tunnel, signalling our proximity to home.

I must have been about nine or ten when my father received a letter from the railway company stating that a report had been sent to them that he was guilty of carrying on a trade outside his work as an employee of the company. My Uncle George received a similar reprimand, and since they were the only men at that time to receive such letters, we knew that we had an enemy in our midst. We were never told the name of the person who made the report to the company, but it was not difficult to guess the source. Shortly afterwards, a little virago of a woman, the wife of a railwayman, appeared at our door and hurled insults at my dear, gentle mother. I greatly admired the courage with which mother stood up to the onslaught, and there was a truly dramatic ending to the encounter when mother sent the enemy packing with the gypsy's warning ringing in her ears, 'Never darken my doorway again!'. Fortunately, she never did.

So my law-abiding and much respected father gave up his innocent pastime and confined his boot and shoe repairing only to the family's needs, but his tools were put to good use during World War II when he held classes for the older evacuees in the village, and taught them the rudiments of the trade. For me, this incident was perhaps a salutary lesson, for it taught me that in my small world, hitherto so serene and pleasant, other forces were at work. It is something we all have to learn, sooner or later.

Meanwhile, as a pupil in Mr Cobley's class, I learned under his skilful teaching to conquer algebra, though mathematics was never my favourite subject. Truth to tell, I, a slow learner, must have been a disappointment to him, for three years previously my sister Margaret had been a pupil in his class. Highly intelligent, bright and receptive, she had been a model pupil, and was awarded a County Scholarship at the age of eleven.

We were, I think, exceedingly fortunate in having Mr Cobley as our headmaster, for he was a dedicated teacher. A strict disciplinarian. he brooked no nonsense from his pupils, and we were very much in awe of him. Yet he had his lighter side for he was very fond of poetry, and his dramatic renderings of his favourite poems delighted us all. I can still remember every word of *He fell among thieves*. His younger daughter Joyce was a friend of my sister, and there were never to be forgotten parties at his house when he showed another side of his character, organising games and romping with us like any ordinary father.

The results Mr Cobley obtained from us in the Eleven Plus examinations were remarkable for a village school. In the year when I won my 'Free Place' to the local High School at Brackley no less than six of us were similarly successful,

A series of view from my days at Brackley High School 1928-1935. *Top left:* A school group, I am third from left, back row. *Top right:* With my friend Joan Milsom. *Centre:* New school uniform. *Above:* I am third from right as a cross-gartered Malvolio in Shakespeare's *Twelfth Night.* *(All) Ruth Irons' Collection*

four of us going on to become teachers in due course. A 'Free Place' meant that tuition fees and travelling expenses were paid by the authorities. Some families of small means were also given an allowance towards school uniform, but father, by then a locomotive driver, was considered able to bear the cost himself.

The boys who had obtained scholarships went to Towcester Grammar School, and the girls to Brackley High School, some 14 miles from Woodford. We travelled by train, under the strict supervision of prefects, for a few years before I started there as a pupil, a girl from the village had been killed when a carriage door was inadvertently opened and she fell on the line. In any case, apart from the safety angle, bad behaviour on our part would have been quickly reported to the school's headmistress by the first class bowler-hatted commuters who boarded the train *en route* for Marylebone. On the long walk to and from the station to school we walked in a decorous crocodile through the town, conscious always that we must do nothing to damage the good name of the school.

I wish that I could report that I, daughter of a father who valued education highly, had made the most of the opportunities offered me during my five years at the school. I did fairly well in English, my favourite subject, and I revelled in the school library, but history and geography never really came alive for me. This is strange, for all my adult life I have read travel and history books for pleasure, and my hobby for many years has been the study and recording of local history, yet so it was. Nor can I report success in the gymnasium and on the playing field, for physical prowess was never my forte. Yet it was a good school with a dedicated staff under the diminutive head mistress, Miss Whitehead. I can see her now in her beautifully tailored suit and immaculate shingled grey hair, as she made her entry into the hall for school assembly.

It was entirely in keeping with my still imaginative view of life that my greatest moments of happiness came when I took part in the end of term plays we performed. On the stage, and before a receptive audience, all inhibitions vanished, and I had no difficulty in taking on the identity of the character I played. There was one glorious moment when I had performed as a cross-gartered Malvolio in *Twelfth Night*, and one of the governors of the school called me to him and said, 'If my daughter could act as well as you have just done, I should feel bound to send her to Drama School'. My dear father had the unwelcome task of telling me, kindly but firmly, that a future on the stage was not for me - the daughter of a railwayman earning her living as a professional actress - unthinkable! Sir Peter Hall, son of a station master, had not at that time risen to fame, but alas, it would not have made any difference to my father's decision.

So after matriculation it was the teaching profession for me. Two of my friends went on to a training college in London and two of us taught as uncertificated teachers, as one could in those days. University was not really an option for us, but in the following year, a former pupil from the council school, Gerald Pratt did go on from his training college to university and obtained a science degree, the first son of a railwayman in our village to be thus honoured.

Incidentally, my college years, of which I have the happiest memories, came a few years later, for at the age of 18 I was engaged to be married to a young teacher at the village school, and it seemed as though an early marriage would

The Medieval Parish Church of St Mary the Virgin. A tombstone on the right of the path bears this charming epitaph 'William Marriott, Poet, Singer, Thatcher. Died 1871, aged 77'.

Ruth Irons' Collection

The interior of the church. In the north wall there is a niche containing the stone effigy of a lady thought to be that of Maud Holland, Lady of the Manor in 1330. *Ruth Irons' Collection*

be in store for me. Sadly, my fiancé contracted tuberculosis and died of the disease at an early age.

One thing I remember vividly from my college days is that when I came home during vacations, bursting with my newfound knowledge, my father could discuss with me on equal terms many of the subjects I was studying. I was amazed at his wide knowledge gained from the books he studied, and it gave me pleasure, at the end of my college days, to lay at his feet two small triumphs, namely a prize for the best written work of my year, and an A grade in Education.

Church and Chapel

It would be naive of me to suggest that all members of our society were God-fearing, and that individually we were not guilty of some of the sins that mankind is heir to, but in point of fact, the spiritual needs of the parish were amply provided for in the four churches that existed. The Anglican Church of St Mary the Virgin had been established since Norman times, and in the 18th and 19th centuries during the great evangelical revival, groups of Methodists and other non-conformists such as the Moravians had held meetings in the parish. With the coming of the railway and the sudden increase in the population, provision was made to house the swelling congregations, and in 1902 the Methodists built a large chapel at Hinton, followed by the Moravians in 1906 in Parsons Street. In 1912 a small Catholic church was provided at Hinton, to serve the parish and neighbouring villages.

So, all denominations were catered for, and it is interesting to note that in the main, old farming families and those long-established favoured the Anglican church, while among the railway fraternity there were many non-conformists, and only a small number of Catholics. My family attended the Moravian church, and I remember how when a stranger asked me my religious persuasion, and I replied that I was a Moravian, a slightly speculative and guarded expression crossed the face of the person to whom I imparted the information. It was as if my family and I were suspected of some crankish leaning towards a strange religious sect.

It is understandable that many people would have known nothing about the Moravians, and of John Hus (*c.*1370-1415), the Bohemian founder of the church, who was martyred in 1415 for making public his dissatisfaction with some of the practices of the Roman Catholic church. Yet John Hus and his followers were in reality the forerunners of the Reformation, and the Moravian Church has the distinction of being the oldest non-conformist church in Northern Europe.

We forget in these modern times when church attendance is diminishing, the important part that church life had for many people in village communities, and no account of my childhood experiences could be complete without some mention of it.

I have thought often, in my adult life during my excursions into Europe, that the builders of the Moravian Church at Woodford must have consciously or unconsciously had in mind the structure of the small churches one sees perched on the hillsides or in the valleys of Austria. Our church, stone-built, had a small bell tower with a conical red tiled roof. Behind it was the burial ground where all the gravestones were flat slabs in accordance with Moravian custom.

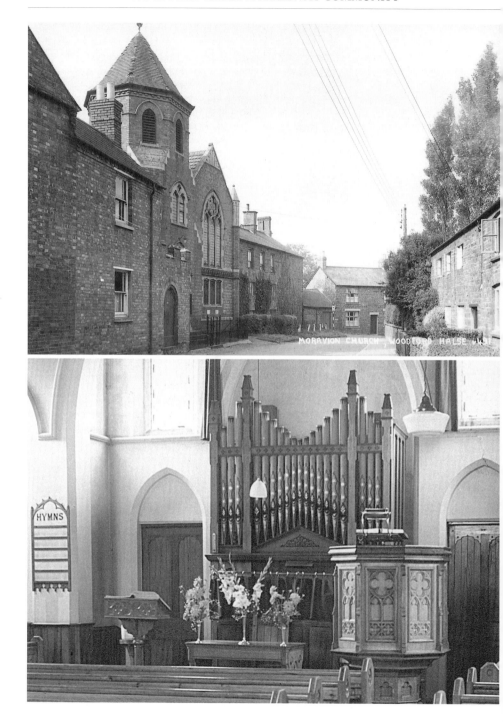

Above: The Methodist chapel at Hinton.
Top left: The Moravian Church in Parsons Street. Father was a lay preacher there.
Bottom left: The interior of the Moravian Church at Woodford Halse. The Moravian church originated in Bohemia, its founder John Hus (1370-1415) having been deeply influenced by the English reformer John Wycliffe. John Hus was martyred in 1415, being burnt at the stake as a 'heretic'.
Below: The Roman Catholic Church of St Joseph's in Hinton.   *(All) Ruth Irons' Collection*

I loved the interior of the church with its stained glass windows and shiny pine pews. At the end of every pew there used to be a barley sugar brass handle with a metal tray underneath to hold walking sticks and umbrellas, and though we were never in the habit of kneeling to pray, some of the pews sported cushions for the old and infirm to sit upon. Best of all, I loved the circular window over the altar table with the ancient emblem of Christendom, the lamb with the flag, and round it the Moravian motto in Latin, *Vicit Agnus Noster Eum Sequaver*.

Our conception of beauty is a very personal thing and changes with the years, but in my early childhood not only the building itself, but many events connected with that church, brought me so much innocent joy. The annual Sunday School outing for instance, when we were taken by horse and cart to a nearby farm, there to picnic in the fields and play boisterous games. The crowning moment was when our superintendent took a box of sweets, and like the sower of olden times threw them far and wide, carefully avoiding the cow pats, and we scrambled for them among the grasses.

The annual Sunday School Christmas party was another highlight not just because of the presents we received, but because on these occasions a huge fir tree was installed on the platform in the school room and on the end of every branch there was a real wax candle. We waited with baited breath while Mr Welch, the superintendent, carefully lit each one, with his daughter Lucy standing by with a wet sponge in case of accidents. The lights in the schoolroom were then dimmed, and when the tree was ablaze with light, we sang *Jesus bids us shine with a pure, clear light*. It was a wonderful moment.

Impressive too, was when, in accordance with Moravian custom, we rose early on Easter Sunday morning and walked in procession to the small burial ground at the back of the church, to celebrate with hymns and prayers the Resurrection of our Lord. I am sure that for a small child such experiences had no deep religious significance, but it was exciting to walk along the deserted streets on our way to and from church.

By the standards of today, the restrictions imposed upon church-goers in our village in the years before World War II, seem, in retrospect, fairly rigorous. It was not done to frequent public houses, use bad language, gamble, garden, or do household tasks like the laundry on the Sabbath day, and promiscuity in sexual matters was a sin. Of course there were lapses, human nature being what it is, but generally speaking the God-fearing members of the population led remarkably upright and decent lives.

Entertainment

But life in our village was not all concerned with hard work and religious observance - far from it! We never lacked for entertainment, and I think it was remarkable that in a community where there was a good deal of shift work, events were organised and carried through with enthusiasm and with great enjoyment for all concerned.

In most industrialised societies of the latter 19th and 20th century, music making in the form of a brass band was one outlet for amateur performers, and we were no exception. The Woodford Brass Band played at many functions - the Remembrance Sunday Service round the war memorial, at the aforementioned Hospital Sunday Services in the Parson's Close, and of course at the fetes and flower shows where the cheerful sounds emanating from the shining brass instruments put us all in a festive mood.

Then there was the Red and White Concert Party, with entertainers culled in the main from the Methodists, not surprising perhaps, since this church has a strong musical tradition, dating from the rousing hymns written by its founders, the brothers Wesley. Mr Hopley was the violinist, and his wife Louise the pianist and singer. There was no lack of male voices to render solos and the occasional quartet. Mr Billy Preece, our favourite performer, was a born comedian and he had merely to walk on the platform wearing a funny hat to reduce us to helpless giggles.

Members from our church, the Moravians, were strong on performances of operettas, produced by Miss Clark a teacher at the village school. Once, when such a work had an oriental setting, my father constructed in our back yard the framework of an elephant which he covered with canvas. I was very impressed by his ingenuity, and even more so when on another occasion he improvised a variety show including a waxwork exhibition with live models, who frequently broke down into giggles when exposed to the public gaze. As Master of Ceremonies, father borrowed for this performance, a top hat and tails, and very distinguished he looked!

But our entertainments were not all, as it were, home-made, for we had the Hippodrome, an establishment which could only have been brought into being in a newly-formed community by some imaginative entrepreneur with an eye to business. It always reminded me of the places of entertainment opened up in the Middle-West of America for the new inhabitants of cowboy country, for it had a somewhat temporary appearance. Erected in 1921, the Hippodrome was intended for a cinema showing silent films, but when the Saville brothers took over the building in the middle 1920s it was also the venue for live performances by travelling companies. My most vivid memory of those times is of a somewhat raucous rendering of 'I dillied, I dallied . . .' by a lady carrying a stuffed parrot in a cage. I thought it was wonderful. It was my first taste of live theatre with professional artists performing before footlights, third rate perhaps, but to my uncritical eye, entirely magical.

The silent films we saw there had Miss Connie Saville at the piano to set the atmosphere for the film action. My friend Edith, who later became headmistress of a small village school, told me that when she was pianist at morning assemblies, she never rose from her stool, and still playing, admonished an unruly pupil over the piano lid, without being reminded of Miss Saville's ability to quell an unruly audience while playing a spirited rendering of the *Zampa Overture*, as cowboys and Indians galloped over the horizon.

Alas, the Hippodrome was badly damaged by fire in 1934 and closed as a place of entertainment, but nothing daunted, the Saville Brothers then built a small cinema, the Savoy, in Church street, and there, to our wonder and delight, the first talkie films were shown. People came from the villages of Byfield, Preston and Eydon and the cinema was always filled to capacity at weekends. I remember how just as a film was reaching its climax, Miss Saville would walk down the aisle

The Woodford Brass Band which entertained at many functions.   *Ruth Irons' Collection*

Woodford's 'Kazoo' Band formed about 1910.   *Ruth Irons' Collection*

A Moravian operetta with an Eastern flavour. My sister is standing third from right in the front row. Father constructed the model elephant. *Ruth Irons' Collection*

A Moravian missionary pageant, myself as the cheerful cleric in the centre.
Ruth Irons' Collection

The Red and White Concert party. The lady in the centre of the front row is Mrs Marriot Hopley, a gifted amateur musician, and my teacher in the infants' school.   *Ruth Irons' Collection*

The Hippodrome, Woodford Halse, where live variety shows were staged, and the first silent films made their debut.   *Ruth Irons' Collection*

whispering the summons, 'Eydon bus! Eydon bus!', and shadowy figures rose, and stumbling over our feet in the darkness, and with many a backward glance at the screen, left for their transport home. In the 1960s, with the advent of television, the Savoy cinema ceased to function, and the building was bought by the Anglican church to serve as a Church Hall, replacing the old corrugated hut known as the 'Tin Tabernacle' where formerly social functions were held.

When the ex-servicemen's hall was built in 1928, it became for the village the main social centre. It had the distinction of being the first public building in Woodford to have electricity, for this amenity came just in time for the opening of the hall. The building was heated by two large coke stoves and had three billiard tables in constant use. The hall was the venue for meetings, whist drives, dances and concerts. I recall that it was there I had my first taste of music performed by professional musicians. Miss Hayes, the daughter of our village doctor, was a cellist, and sometimes she brought to the hall for a concert some of her friends who were professional musicians. I knew at once, young as I was, that here was music of a different order, not just rendered for entertainment but with a life of its own, disciplined and to me, very beautiful.

The dances that were held in the hall would seem to the young people of today, very tame affairs, with no loud disco music and flashing lights. The music was often provided by a visiting band. The Daventry Syncopaters were very popular. Their repertoire for the waltzes and foxtrots was not conducive to abandoned movements by the dancers, though occasionally the older members at the gathering did let their hair down in a spirited performance of the Lancers. It was all, as I remember, very innocent fun. There were certain rules to be observed - no unseemly behaviour in the hall, and no going outside with a partner while the dance was in progress. Very occasionally, one or two males who had imbibed too freely at one of the local pubs caused a disturbance, but they were quickly ejected by the caretaker and Master of Ceremonies, and all fights were settled outside.

It was all very informal, for whereas married or courting couples went with their partners, young people attended the dances with their friends, and were safely escorted home in groups at the end of the evening. I doubt if much sexual promiscuity went on, for girls valued their virginity in those days, and the number of unmarried mothers in the parish could be counted on the fingers of one hand. There were some couples who had to get married because of impending births, but it was not usually the consequence of casual sex, but the result of long standing relationships.

It would be easy, in retrospect, to sentimentalise about the good old days, but in matters of social and moral behaviour the children growing up in my village at that time were spared many of the temptations that youngsters face today. There was no drug abuse or teenage alcoholism, and though the railway families came from many diverse backgrounds, there was full employment, and the modest wages, so hardly earned, did not admit extravagant behaviour. The railway company was a stern, but fair employer, and the work imposed its own discipline on the men and their families.

Hinton Wesleyan Cricket club 1921.   *Ruth Irons' Collection*

Woodford Central FC, league champions in the Brackley & District league 1920-1921.
Ruth Irons' Collection

Holidays and Travel

I always think of myself country-born, but in truth our lives were very different from the normal experience of children born in some remote Northamptonshire village. When, during our rambles along the country lanes, we came upon the quiet villages of Eydon, Preston Capes, and my mother's birthplace of Charwelton, it did seem to us that we were invading different worlds. They were so quiet and peaceful, and though they were beautiful, they struck us as rather backward, and lacking all the activity and excitement of a railway village.

We were, in fact, as the children of railwaymen, much travelled, for our fathers were able to obtain one very valuable perk connected with their work - privilege tickets for train journeys. Father made full use of these concessions and we made frequent trips to the neighbouring towns of Banbury, Rugby and Leicester, and more exciting still, visits to London once or twice a year. I never forget father taking me to the National Gallery when I was about 12 years old. I was spellbound, looking at the beautiful works of art, for it was my first experience of, and entry into, a world which has given infinite pleasure all my life.

The crown of the year was the annual seaside holiday. It was not so for all railway families, but we were blessed with a thrifty father who put aside a small sum each week out of his wages, and made it all possible. Not for us, of course, a week at a luxury hotel, or even a guest house, but rooms were hired in an ordinary house, very much like our own. We catered for ourselves, though the landlady cooked for us, and how we managed it I do not know, but our luggage always included some choice vegetables from father's allotment, and a large and delicious fruit cake baked by my mother. It is amusing, in these weight-conscious days, to recall that on the first day of our holiday the family was weighed, and the holiday was considered a success if we all gained a few pounds during the week.

Later on, father grew more adventurous, and still taking advantage of the cheap fares, we travelled to Aberdeen, our first excursion outside England. We went on the night train, and I remember the thrill of crossing the Forth bridge, just as dawn was breaking. During our adolescent years, when we chose to holiday with friends, father took mother several times to Ireland, where she found the sight of armed policemen patrolling the wide Dublin streets, somewhat alarming. Towards the end of his life, mother, whose health was delicate, could no longer manage journeys so far afield, but he had one last holiday in his beloved Scotland with a railwayman friend, and regarded it as one of his crowning achievements that in his fifties he climbed to the top of Ben Nevis - and quenched his thirst with handfuls of snow on the summit of the mountain.

Nothing, in these days of more sophisticated travel by motor car, coach, and by aeroplane, can ever compare with me for the excitement of those early train journeys to the coast, when we, who lived so far inland, steamed into our destination, and caught our first glimpse of the sea .

Right: Kneeling on the left of the photograph, my sister and I (wearing hats) on holiday in Skegness in 1923.
Ruth Irons' Collection

Below: Mother and father on holiday in Scotland in 1933.
Ruth Irons' Collection

Trade Unions and Politics

The company could not have had a better employee than my father, for he was punctilious in the discharge of his duties. He believed in the dignity of labour and that a man should always be worthy of his hire. When, towards the end of his working life, the company promoted him to the post of 'acting oil inspector', his insistence on efficient workmanship was not always popular, but he never lowered the standards he set himself.

Father was a socialist all his adult life. He was keenly interested in politics, and in common with the majority of the railwaymen, he sympathised with the Labour party in its struggle for better conditions of life for the working classes. For us children, elections were exciting events, and never were the differences in social status more evident than on such occasions. Supporters of the Conservative and Liberal parties were definitely in a minority and mostly confined to the farming fraternity who wore their blue rosettes somewhat defiantly as they went to the polling booths. There were a few railwaymen who confessed themselves to be Tories, but they were regarded as disloyal to their class, and possibly social climbers. Masons fell into the same category.

There was a strong trade union movement in the community. Most railwaymen belonged to the National Union of Railwaymen which catered for all grades. I loved their banner which was carried on special occasions. It was illustrated by a colour picture of the man in the fable who bore a bundle of sticks which because of its density could not be broken, as a single stick could have been. Father belonged to the smaller, and we thought more select, Associated Society of Locomotive Engineers and Firemen, the highly-skilled members of the work force.

I think that relations and negotiations between the unions and the railway company must have been, in that relatively new industry, reasonably conducted, for there were very few strikes in my childhood. I do remember the General Strike of 1926 and I have a vivid picture of a blackleg driver and his mate being escorted up the village street by a policeman. There was a large crowd of people, but despite a few jeers and ironic applause, the atmosphere was not a threatening one, and the recalcitrant driver and his mate looked sheepish rather than fearful. The small woman who danced before them clashing a large pair of cymbals added a distinctly dramatic note to the proceedings, and made it a memorable event for us children.

We did hear of a railwayman's wife who got into serious trouble with her husband because she made a journey on a train driven by a blackleg, but she had been visiting relatives and would have been stranded away from home had she not taken the transport available. Apart from such events, and with a few exceptions, I got the impression that members of the unions were not militant, and in a community where there was full employment this is hardly surprising. In the 1930s and 1940s there was never any doubt in the minds of the railwaymen that their's was an industry destined to continue far into the future. No one could ever have imagined that in less than two decades Woodford would cease to be a railway village.

For it really did seem during my childhood that the 'City of the Future' had come into being. Woodford had been extended in the 1920s to include a large

The railwaymen's strike committee, Woodford Halse 1926.   *Ruth Irons' Collection*

council estate always known as the 'New Buildings'. It was situated half a mile from Woodford along the Byfield Road, so children of the railway families living there had a considerable walk to and from the village schools in all weathers, but it was not looked upon as a hardship in those days. There was then no housing shortage, an excellent assortment of shops catered for our material needs, churches, schools, and entertainment facilities were all established making a self-contained, thriving community. Nor were the railwaymen slow to take office on the parish council and thus have a hand in local government. One remarkable family, the Adams', produced future mayors of Manchester and Leicester, and my friend Mr James Anscomb, ever interested in affairs of the parish, became a county councillor and Magistrate, and Justice of the Peace (*see below*).

Father never sought office in local government, in his union, or in the Labour party. His socialism was a very personal thing, expressed in the sharing of his gifts within the enclosed society in which fate had placed him. He was not ambitious in a worldly sense, and although he was well aware of the inequalities of life, and was saddened sometimes by the abuse of privilege by the wealthy and powerful, he was never bitter or envious.

I have before me as I write, a letter sent to my mother after his death by the secretary of his union. 'Those of our fraternity who worked with your husband regard him as their Philosopher and Friend' he wrote - a fitting tribute to someone who gave unstinting service to the community. An abiding memory on the day of the funeral is of how, as we followed his bier conveyed by six of his comrades, we were met at a corner of the village street by a long line of his workmates who filled our small church to overflowing. Later, when Father's obituaries appeared in the local newspapers, there was one personal tribute sent anonymously, from which I quote the following sentence, 'Will Irons', it read, 'was a great hearted, quietly spoken, Christian gentleman', and indeed he was!

Woodford Railwaymen and Local Government

The building of the Great Central Railway through the village and the extensive marshalling yard, locomotive depot and wagon repair shops built to serve the railway, meant employment for a very large number of men and without doubt the impact on local government services in the district was very considerable.

The Highway Board would be concerned with highway diversions and the building of bridges over the public highways and the newly-formed district council with the provision of adequate sewerage for the large number of houses to be erected in the parish, the parish council was faced with all manner of difficulties that the cutting of the line through the parish brought with it.

The parish council held their first meeting in December 1894 and in March 1895 we find them pressing the Postal Authorities for a Postal Order Office in the village. In May they decided to write to Messrs T. Oliver & Sons drawing their attention to the nuisance and danger of their men sleeping in barns and outhouses and asking them to provide accommodation for the men.

However, the coming of the railway brought with it men prepared to do their bit in the local government work of the district and we find that railwaymen were very soon taking part in the affairs of the village as members of the parish council.

So far as I can trace the first railwayman to serve on the parish council was Walter Wills, who was elected to the council in 1899. He is described in the parish Minute book of 1905 as a wagon builder and it is presumed that he would be a railwayman when he first joined the council. In 1901, when the number of councillors was increased from nine to eleven, he was joined by Mr F. Woodcock who later removed to Aylesbury. At the next election both of the above men disappear and we have station master Mr James Coulson as a member. In 1907 he was joined by the locomotive running shed foreman, Mr G.H. Askew, and in 1910 we find the addition of Mr W. Hancock, a signalman.

It was noticed, when searching the columns of the *Northampton Mercury*, that the election of Mr Hancock brought first mention of politics in local parish council elections. The election result was headed, 'Mr Hancock (Socialist) knocks off Mr Bright'. In 1913 there were six railwaymen on the council, three of them signalmen, so there was a majority of railwaymen on the council for the first time.

The first all-railwaymen council appears to be that elected in 1928 and then again in 1946 and 1949 all the councillors were railwaymen with the exception of Mrs Edith Adams JP, who was the widow of a railwayman. Mrs Adams also has the distinction of being one of the first women to be elected to the council, being elected with Mrs G.M. Castleton in March 1934. The *Northampton Mercury* of 9th March, 1934 announced in very large type that women had been elected to the parish council at Woodford Halse for the first time.

Mr Richard Adams, the late husband of Mrs Edith Adams, was one of a family, the boys of which proved to be remarkable in local government affairs. The family, two girls and four boys, Samuel Nelson, Richard, Thomas Henry and A. Frederick, were left orphans at a very early age. The boys, as soon as they were able, joined the railway and all took a keen interest in local government. Samuel and Richard both served on Woodford Parish Council and Frederick on Byfield parish council. Samuel Nelson and Richard also served on the Daventry Rural District Council, and Nelson Avenue on the council house estate was named after Samuel Nelson and Adams Road after Richard, for the part they played in securing sites for the building of these houses. Richard, unfortunately, died in 1935 and his passing was undoubtedly a great loss to local government in the area. Samuel Nelson went to Leicester and served on the city council, at one time being a member of 19 public authorities.

Thomas Henry left the village and went to Manchester, serving on the city council and becoming Lord Mayor in 1946-1947. Frederick, living at Byfield served on the parish council there and made an attempt to enter the county council by contesting the Weedon Bec division in 1922. He later left the district and lived at March.

To serve on the rural district council was a more difficult proposition for a working railwayman as there would not only be the question of getting to the meeting place at Daventry, some nine miles away, but also the difficulty of getting the time off from work. So far as I have been able to trace, it was not until 1928 that any railwayman attempted to get himself elected on to the rural district council and in that year we find that Mr R. Adams and Mr J.T. Bruce made unsuccessful attempts. I have no records of the election of 1931 but in 1934 two railwaymen, Richard Adams and Mr J.H. Goodhand, were elected.

It would appear that the representation of the village on the council was increased from two members to three about 1937 when we find the Hon. Marcus Herbert Pelham elected to the council and remaining there until 1946, elections having been suspended owing the World War II. In 1946 three railwaymen were elected to the council and railwaymen have held all three seats since that time.

If the local railwaymen found it almost an impossibility to serve on the rural district council it was more so with regard to the county council and it is not until 1937 that we find an attempt being made. In that year William Bannard, a locomotive fireman, opposed Capt. the Hon. Marcus Herbert Pelham without success. The result of the contest in the Byfield division, which includes the parish of Woodford, being returned as Pelham 905, Bannard 346. In 1946, when elections were resumed after the war the division was contested by Mr J.W. Anscomb, a railway goods guard, and by Mr A.V. Nicolle of West Farndon with the result that a railwayman represented the division for the first time, J.W. Anscomb being the successful candidate.

It seems that the first Woodford railwayman to be appointed a Justice of the Peace for the county was Samuel N. Adams. Then in 1942 Mrs Edith Adams was appointed, followed in 1946 by Mr A.C. Jordan, a locomotive driver, and then in 1949 Mr J.W. Anscomb, a goods guard, was appointed.

Conclusion

I do not regret, that as the years pass, my visits to my native village grow less frequent, for though many familiar landmarks remain, without the clamour of the busy railway, the place seems strangely silent. Yet, with the precious gift of memory, I can span the years and recreate the Woodford of my childhood. Not least of all the memories that bring me pleasure is the joy I found as a child in the surrounding countryside, unchanged, despite the coming of the railway.

Thus, every springtime, I recall how my sister and I used to gather violets under the hedgerow in Shrimpton's meadow. From the village street we would turn into the steeply banked Kitchen Lane and cross the old wooden bridge over the winding Cherwell stream, to the field where the violets grew in such profusion. And it was by that same route on misty Autumn mornings when my sailor uncle was on leave that we walked to the fields beyond, to gather mushrooms for breakfast. Further afield still, there were the delights of picnics in the park of the great house at Fawsley, and rambles through Badby Woods, so near to my mother's birthplace at Charwelton.

Precious too, are my memories of the home in Castle Road, pervaded always by my mother's gentle presence as she went about her household tasks - she of whom a schoolgirl friend once said, 'The goodness shines from your mother's face!'. My sister Margaret is very like her, for she has inherited all her skills as home-maker, and a loving kindness which has never faltered through all the years of our close relationship.

When I was small, I always thought of my father as a man of immense physical strength, though in reality he was of average height and of a slim build. I suspect that the strength I sensed in him was not physical at all, but came from within, an integrity and firmness of purpose which manifested itself in all he said and did. As I grew older it used to make me sad at times, to see him reading with intense concentration the books which meant so much to him, for such precious moments were all too rare in his busy life. Yet I know that he would not have had things different, for he found in his life as a railwayman every aspect of his work on the steam railway of intense and lasting interest. He shared with his fellow railwaymen an enthusiasm for, and a pride in their part in that great enterprise. It made of them a unique and unified labour force.

Our personal history, our parentage and birthplace, are determined, and have their roots in the past. I am grateful that it was my destiny to be born, and to spend my formative years in a railway village, for like so many, even today, I take a romantic view of the age of the steam railway. It required the labour of many hands to keep those splendid machines and their loads 'on the rails'. The men, who like my father, created out of such work a vigorous, thriving community in that corner of Northamptonshire should never be forgotten. In words borrowed from Gray's Elegy, I raise this trophy to their memory.

The old wooden bridge by which we crossed the Cherwell stream on our way to the fields beyond. *Ruth Irons*

The Home Guard, men of the Nos. 1 and 3 platoons of D Company (Woodford Halse District) of the 10th (Daventry) Battalion celebrate the capture of their quarry in a parachute exercise on 24th October, 1943. The Woodford men, who were armed with an assortment of weapons including rifles and 9 mm sten guns, were commended for their efficiency in this exercise.

Ruth Irons' Collection

Appendix One

Some Recollections of Woodford in the 1940s
by Fred Jeycock

Following the Fall of France and the retreat from Dunkirk in May-June 1940, a company of the 4th/7th Royal Dragoon Guards was billeted in the village, mainly in the stables and tack rooms of the Gorse Hotel and White Hart Hotel which were large buildings for a small village, rooms that were unused in these 'pubs' were taken over for men and other needs, the company remaining approximately three years until the second front. The soldiers were badly equipped, through no fault of their own, but they were a very friendly group, and were soon accepted into the community.

After industry went onto a 'Total war' footing the 4th/7th had better equipment, they were armed with large tanks, which of course needed 'hard standing', so one of farmer 'Cam' Douglas' rickyards was concreted and an area alongside the River Cherwell near the railway station received the same treatment, and may still be in the same condition.

May 1940 saw the formation of the Local Defence Volunteers (soon renamed the Home Guard) all over Britain, and Woodford had a contingent. Mr Tom Coy the yardmaster's clerk was made commanding officer and I believe he attained the rank of major. Goods guard 'Danny' Long was made an officer, but not all railwaymen at the depot were so keen - it interfered with sleeping time for many on shiftwork. However, if the need had arisen I feel sure they would have been where they were needed.

I am not too sure of the year, I think it was 1942, a hostel was built on the Byfield Road and staffed by ladies of the Land Army, they originated from various parts of Britain, mainly from the north of the country, they worked on local farms, drank their beer, married some of the local lads, one or two are still living in the village.

Concrete 'hard standing' for the tanks of the 4th/7th Dragoon Guards at 'Cam' Douglas' rickyard in Hinton. *Ruth Irons' Collection*

Talking of beer, there were four pubs including the two hotels, the Gorse, the White Hart, the Fleur-de-Lys and the Hare and Hounds. The 'Fleur' remains, the Gorse Hotel is now a club, the other two ceased trading.

Being a village 60-odd miles from London we had a large number of evacuees billeted on most households, we were reasonably safe but we did have a few bombs but luckily no casualties, the railway was probably the target. Makeshift schools had to be provided as the two schools of the village could not cope, church rooms were used. Teachers from London were with the children so things seemed to go along fine.

Railway work can be a very dangerous way of earning a living. Permanent Way men have 'look-outs' when working on the track, working in a marshalling yard one has to be vigilant regarding incoming and outgoing trains, plus wagons being shunted into various sidings. At Woodford I can recall several cases where men received injuries which were not fatal, however a year or two after the war a fatality occurred to goods guard Bill Scott who was a single man, very popular with everyone both at work and away from it. After crossing the Up Loop Line he was hit by an Up Express when making his way along the slope leading to the station platform, it may have been the 'Master Cutler' which ran over the ex-Great Central line in those days. This accident really cast a shadow over everyone that knew and worked with Bill.

'Windcutters' or 'Runners' were introduced between Annesley (north of Nottingham) and Woodford during the summer of 1947. Annesley trainmen joined the trains at Bulwell Common after being ferried from Annesley on a shuttle service. For many years particularly during the war years a change-over system had existed, change-over of crews generally being done at Leicester Goods. However, the 'Runners' were worked through to Woodford by Annesley men.

On arrival at Woodford, the Annesley men were diagrammed to be relieved by Woodford men, who were required to take the engine into the 'Loco', turn it ready for its return on the 'Down Road', fill the tender with water, and make sure of an adequate supply of coal was on board. After the change-over system, this did not go down well with the Woodford men who would not accept the new methods and initially refused to co-operate. The 'Runner' service was a great success, savings of time and manpower were achieved. As a small compensation, Woodford men were given similar workings between Woodford and Neasden but not on the same scale, as the traffic was less numerous.

Wartime shortages of most everyday things, such as cigarettes, alcohol, razor blades even, Brylcreem and tinned goods, temptation seemed to be at hand especially with Government Stores labelled as being in some wagons. A group of yard staff at Woodford succumbed to temptation but after a time were caught and punished. Their previous good names tarnished and the honesty of the village degraded, time of course did heal those concerned. With the loss of yard staff, those that were not involved had to work twelve hours a shift for many months until more staff were recruited, mainly from Leicester.

The sign of the Fleur-de-Lys.   *Ruth Irons' Collection*

Appendix Two

The Last Passenger Train from Woodford
by Cyril Jordan

It was a black day for Woodford Halse on Saturday, September 3rd, 1966 when the last passenger trains ran and many railway enthusiasts from around the district were on the station, and off it, with cameras and note books taking photos and engine numbers for the last time at Woodford Halse station. Many old railwaymen, wives and children were present including some men and women who when very young were taken from the School to see the first passenger train to stop in the station on its way to Marylebone in March, 1898. Also to see the then Vicar of Woodford, the Revd F. A. Smith, buy the first ticket from the booking office, and there, on behalf of the Parish Council, present the Railway Directors with a Council resolution thanking them for the railway coming through Woodford Halse Parish. It was the means of finding work for many of the children present, on the railway instead of on the farm. This very many did and worked in the locomotive sheds, traffic departments, carriage and wagon shop, and the wagon sheet repair shop.

Many houses were built for men being transferred to Woodford from other depots on the old Great Central Railway. Families arrived to find no proper roads, no proper footpaths and the village all in darkness, except for a few lights on the station and shunting yard. What a great change to village life took place after these families arrived. Church and Chapel began to fill and new ones had to be built for Methodists and Moravians, also a new mixed school adjoined the old Church School. Men and women soon took interest in the village life and eventually two brass bands formed, and an orchestra under the conductorship of the family Doctor Alex Glen Hayes.

Churches had full choirs, football and cricket clubs formed, and local flower and vegetable for shows were held. Then following the first war a large army hut was erected and became the Picture Palace. Eventually this was not large enough and a new building was erected and is now the Parish Church Hall. The gas works followed in the village and soon the Parish Council got street lighting. Now it's all gone and men have found work in Banbury, Daventry, Chipping Warden and other places.

Some old engine drivers were very sad on the Saturday evening when they heard for the last time in Woodford 'The footplatemen's chorus'. Tips from the guard on his whistle, and a toot from the engine whistle, driver opens the regulator and listens with his fireman as they move from station, the engine singing 'I think I shall, I think I shall', until the regulator closes and then follows 'I've done it, I've done it'.

Several old drivers turned of away with lumps in their throats and tears in their eyes to think of never hearing the old beloved steam engines in Woodford, or a train again singing its song and chorus.

* * * * * * * * * * *

The above report was written by Cyril Jordan, who spent all his working life on the railways at Woodford, he had a fine tenor voice and was a member of the Methodist choir as well as the Red and White Concert Party. He, along with the young lady who was to become Mrs Jordan, saw the first train in Woodford in March 1898, and they were both present on the same spot 68 years later, to see the departure of the last passenger train from Woodford station.

Two views of the Woodford breakdown train, showing the steam crane in action, and the interior of the mess van which accompanied the crane. *(Both) D. Jackson Collection*

Thomson 'L1' class 2-6-4T No. 67771 waits at Woodford on a southbound train.
D. Matthews/R. Palmer Collection

BR Standard class '9F' 2-10-0 No. 92074 taking water at Woodford Halse on 4th March, 1961.
G.B. Wise

English Electric 0-6-0 diesel shunter No. D3068 shunts wagons in the down yard at Woodford Halse on 4th March, 1961. *Revd G.B. Wise*

'WD' class 2-8-0 No. 90563 approaches Woodford Halse station with a freight for the Banbury line on 4th March, 1961. The terraced houses of the railway village can be seen to the right. *Revd G.B. Wise*

Ex-LMS class '4MT' 2-6-0 No. 43106 on a southbound trip freight at Woodford Halse on 4th March, 1961. *Revd G.B. Wise*

A general view of Charwelton, showing the goods yard on the right, and the standard GCR signal box to the left. *D. Jackson Collection*

The approaches to Woodford Halse, looking south towards Marylebone in the 1960s. *Chris Chesterman*

Track lifting operation at Woodford Halse after the closure of the line.   *Chris Chesterman*

The scene at Woodford locomotive sheds after the removal of the track.   *Chris Chesterman*